Brandywine

Haunts of Southeastern Pennsylvania

Laurie Hull

Schiffer Publishing Ltd

4880 Lower Valley Road, Atglen, Pennsylvania 19310

Designed by Stephanie Daugherty
Type set in :A Charming Font Expanded/
NewBskvll BT

ISBN: 978-0-7643-3041-4

Printed in China

Schiffer Books are available at special discounts for bulk purchases for sales promotions or premiums. Special editions, including personalized covers, corporate imprints, and excerpts can be created in large quantities for special needs. For more information contact the publisher:

Published by Schiffer Publishing Ltd.
4880 Lower Valley Road
Atglen, PA 19310
Phone: (610) 593-1777; Fax: (610) 593-2002
E-mail: Info@schifferbooks.com

Please visit our web site catalog at
www.schifferbooks.com

We are always looking for people to write books on new and related subjects. If you have an idea for a book, please contact us at the above address.

This book may be purchased from the publisher. Include $5.00 for shipping. Please try your bookstore first. You may write for a free catalog. In Europe, Schiffer books are distributed by:
Bushwood Books
6 Marksbury Ave.
Kew Gardens
Surrey TW9 4JF
England
Phone: 44 (0)208 392-8585
Fax: 44 (0)208 392-9876
E-mail: Info@bushwoodbooks.co.uk

Website: www.bushwoodbooks.co.uk
Free postage in the UK. Europe: air mail at cost.
Try your bookstore first.

Dedication

Dedicated to the ghosts that walk among us; may they find peace.

Acknowledgements

My husband, Pauric, and my daughters Aarika, Shannon, and Kira, who were a constant source of encouragement and who are sometimes forced to accompany me and help me in my search for ghosts; Dinah, for her endless patience with me; Carol, for standing out in the freezing cold in cemeteries with me at night, and all of the people in this book who were willing to share their experiences with me.

Contents

Chapter 1

A Word About Ghosts

Since you have picked up and opened this book, I am going to assume that you have at least an interest in ghosts and the paranormal. Maybe you are not sure that ghosts exist. Maybe you believe in them completely. If you do, then you are not alone. According to the 2003 Harris Poll, "51% of the public… believe in ghosts."

So what are ghosts? There are internet sites, books, TV, and radio broadcasts dedicated to the discussion and exploration of hauntings. What causes a ghost? Why do some places get haunted and others don't?

After all my research, I have come to the conclusion that ghosts themselves are an anomaly and no one really *knows* what they are. There are thousands of theories to explain ghosts. The earliest recorded ghost story is from Ancient Greece, so ghosts have been a part of human experience since before the time of Christ. Are they part of our world or does their world intersect ours? Are they human? What are they made of and why do some people see them while others don't?

Most people will tell you that ghosts can be seen by people who are "sensitive" or "psychic" and that ghosts are referred to as *place memory* or the spirits of dead people. This theory holds that the spirit or soul of a person leaves the body at death and then either chooses to stay here or gets stuck somehow and becomes a ghost. Sometimes the ghost is aware of its state and sometimes it seems to be unaware of the passage of the time since its body's death, or even of the fact that it is, indeed, dead! Associated with this idea is the theory that a ghost needs to be released or encouraged to move on to its proper place or state of existence in the afterlife. These ghosts communicate and interact with people, especially psychic ones, and often remain in places that were important to them in life. I refer to these as "intelligent hauntings" because the ghost behaves in a way that suggests some intelligence governing its actions. Not all ghosts fit in this category.

There are accounts of ghostly activity that appear to be more like a video recording that plays over and over again in the same place. In these cases, the ghost does not interact with or respond to the presence of a human being. These types of haunting are "residual hauntings." A good example of this type of haunting is the haunted gallery at Hampton Court in England. In this haunting, which has been reported for the past 450 years, the image of Catherine Howard is seen and heard as she runs screaming down the gallery to plead for her life. This spirit has never been known to interact with any witness and has never done anything but run screaming down the gallery. These types of haunting are believed to be a type of recording on the atmosphere of a place, which is activated by some unknown stimulus. The stimulus causes the recording to play and it is witnessed. This could be the anniversary of the death, the event, or certain weather conditions. It may also be triggered by the presence of someone who is able to see or perceive the recording.

In addition to the two types mentioned above, there is also the appearance of a deceased loved one or friend who appears shortly after death or in a time of great crisis to a living person. Although there are no accounts of this type in this book, this is the kind of spirit most people are likely to encounter. These are often referred to as "warning" or "crisis apparitions". They appear once or twice, give their message of warning or hope, and then are not seen again.

Finally, there is the type of haunting that is the most controversial. This is the haunting involving a non-human entity. This category includes poltergeists, elementals, demons, and any type of spirit presence that was never alive. Some people think that all hauntings are of this type. Others believe that this type of haunting does not exist. I can say that although in the beginning of my investigative career I was unsure about whether these spirits existed, I am now convinced that they do. They are the most dangerous type of spirit to encounter and the most difficult to resolve. They not only interact with humans, but seem to take particular delight in frightening, controlling, and harming them. If you encounter a spirit that deliberately scares you or others, tries to control people's actions, makes demands, or harms them physically or emotionally, please get help immediately from your clergyperson or a professional who is experienced in dealing with his type of phenomena.

I am sure that there are categories that are not listed here. This book is not meant to be a comprehensive study of different types of hauntings. Instead, it is written as a means of sharing experiences that I and others have had, in the hopes that you, the reader, will see a glimpse of that shadowy world of ghosts that may exist in any suburban neighborhood anywhere. Without a doubt, where there are people, there are ghosts!

Chapter 2

A Word About Psychic Abilities

I can't remember a time when I was not aware that we share this world with ghosts. As a child, I often saw and conversed with deceased family members and people that no one else could see or hear. My family and friends were surprised at my knowledge of places and their histories. Most of the time, they just assumed I had read it in a book. Although I was quite a reader, I was getting the information from a truly primary source—the ghosts that still lived in the places.

I must say that my interpretation of what I sense is not always 100% accurate. I am human and my perception is clouded by my own beliefs and ideas. Sometimes the things I "get" are so off the wall that I don't say anything about them to anyone. When this happens I want to kick myself because I always find out later that my sense was right on.

For example, a woman called me to come to her sister's house because they thought it was haunted. I always ask people not to tell me anything about the haunting or the history because I don't want to be influenced in any way. I prefer to just go in cold and let my senses lead me to what is there. So, I arrived with no information about the nature of the haunting.

When I arrived, I kept seeing an image of a white, fluffy cat in my mind. In addition, I kept thinking of King Arthur. I said to myself, *I can't just say I see a white cat and King Arthur! That sounds stupid.* So, I just told them that I kept thinking of King Arthur. They didn't really understand what that could relate to, so I concentrated again. This time I saw pink flowers. I could almost smell them. When I told them about the pink flowers, they again looked at me blankly. *Strike three*, I thought to myself. I suggested that maybe it wasn't a good time and offered to try another time. They agreed, but as I was leaving, the image of the white cat wouldn't leave me alone, so I just said it. "You know, I keep seeing a fluffy white cat." They both stopped at looked at each other. "That's her!" exclaimed the sister, "That's Guinevere!" *Well*, I thought, *there's the King Arthur connection.*

Turns out the woman's mother had a white cat named Guinevere that she had loved dearly. It was her recently deceased mother who she believed was in the house. I asked again about the pink flowers, but that didn't go anywhere. It wasn't until later that night that we found out what the pink flowers meant. The woman called me and asked me what kind of pink flowers I saw. "Roses," I said, "I could almost smell them." She gasped in surprise, "I knew it! I just thought to ask you…well, our mother's name was Rose."

Why didn't I get that? I don't know. The images that I see in my mind are often like a slide show. Sometimes pieces of the picture are missing or blurry. The images often flash by, disjointed, till I can focus on one and hold it in my mind's eye. As I concentrate, the image will become clearer. There are times when I actually see things visually and hear things audibly, but most of the time it is just the pictures, sometimes accompanied by ideas that just pop into my head that I know did not come from me.

Not all people experience spirits the same way I do. We are all individuals and have our own way of connecting with the world or worlds around us. Please enjoy the following accounts of experiences that I and others have had with the spirit world. They all happened exactly as I describe in these pages. The only changes I have made are to names of people and places when requested to do so.

Chapter 3

Brandywine Battlefield

A September 11th in 1777

I would like to begin by setting the record straight. The Battle of Brandywine did not happen on the grounds of the Battlefield Park. It happened in the fields and gardens of the farms all along Birmingham and Wylie Roads in Chadds Ford. There is an excellent driving tour at http://www.ushistory.org/brandywine/drivingtour/car3.htm, where you can follow the progress of the battle as it wound its way through the Brandywine valley.

The tour describes how the British and Hessian soldiers were camped to the East on the ground now occupied by the Radley Run Estates. The American line was formed on a ridge south of the Quaker Meeting House that is still standing today on Birmingham Road. As the British line advanced, skirmishes broke out all along Birmingham Road and in the fields of what is now Fair Meadows Farm.

At the Quaker Meeting House, there is a low stone wall. Today this wall separates the meeting house garden from the Lafayette Cemetery. The American rebels used this wall for cover as they tried to hold back the advancing British line. It didn't work. The Americans were pushed back towards their own line. At the intersection of Wylie Road, the heaviest fighting took place, as the Americans tried desperately to hold their position by firing their cannons at the British army. They were able to decimate one regiment of British soldiers almost completely, but it was not enough. The Americans were forced to retreat all the way back to Route 1 and then to Chester. There were considerable numbers of wounded on both sides in this—the largest land battle of the Revolutionary War.

The minute book of the Birmingham Friends for September 11, 1777 contains the following entry, notable for its irony:

"Today there was much confusion outside."

The meeting house was used as a temporary hospital for the wounded, as were many other structures in the area. The toll for the Americans was heavy and disheartening. After this battle, the British continued their advance north and took Philadelphia two weeks later.

The echoes of this battle can still be felt today. There are constant reminders as you travel through the area. As you explore the area, you will see markers commemorating the brave efforts of Lafayette, Pulaski, Taylor, and McClellan. The monuments to Pulaski, Taylor, and McClellan are found towering over the entry road to the Birmingham-Lafayette Cemetery. A sad reminder of the devastation of that long-ago September 11th is located between the cemetery and the meeting house, in what is now a peace garden. This common grave contains the remains of dead soldiers from both sides of the battle, united in death as they were not able to be in life.

Reports of ghostly British and American soldiers abound in this area. Soldiers have been seen along the roadsides and in the fields on Birmingham and Wylie Roads, especially during foggy weather. This is interesting, because the morning of the battle was very foggy. Cars driving along these roads have seen figures carrying muskets emerge from the mist, cross the road, and vanish on the other side.

During battle reenactments, the spirits have been known to join in, often in search of their regiment. At http://www.ghosttoghost.com/, a re-enactor named Mark reported:

> *"I have been a Revolutionary War re-enactor for nearly thirty years. During the reenactment of the battle, about four years ago, there was a lull in the action. My artillery crew and myself were standing off to one side by a marsh. We noticed movement in the marsh and figured some of our fellows were coming in. Out of this marsh walked a young boy, about sixteen to eighteen years old. His uniform was worn and dirty and he stunk like rotten vegetation. He asked about his unit but was hard to understand as he was speaking in true eighteenth-century English. He also seemed to have a speech problem. We directed him to the area where the unit was and, as he walked away, he vanished. We just stood there looking at each other and asking, 'You saw that, too, right?' To this day we have no idea who he may have been other than casualty in the American War for Independence."*

In my searches for information about the ghosts of the Brandywine Battlefield, I often came across references to General Anthony Wayne as well as an unnamed headless horseman. While it is true that General Anthony Wayne was at the Battle of Brandywine, reports of his ghost at this battlefield are completely unsubstantiated and the claims that his ghost still roams the back roads and fields of Birmingham are probably just legend. As for the horseman, that is likely a case of mistaken location, as there are two other well-documented headless horsemen ghosts in the area that date from the Revolution. One is from the Battle of Cooch's Bridge just over the Delaware /Pennsylvania border, and the other is at the site of the Paoli Massacre in Malvern, Pennsylvania.

Anthony Wayne was a colorful historical figure and well-known soldier of the American Revolution who *did* live in this area. As with George Washington, many locations claim that he lived, stayed, or enjoyed spending time there. The General Wayne Inn in Merion, Pennsylvania was even named after him.

Although he was at this battle, he was at many battles during his career, and there was nothing that occurred at this particular battle that would cause one to think that his spirit would choose to remain there to the exclusion of all of the other battles he participated in. Although I would love to say that his ghost

still haunts this area, it is just not so. His ghost is, however, known to haunt his gravesite at St. David's Episcopal Church in Radnor, Pennsylvania.

I have visited the site of the Battle of Brandywine and followed the course of the battle many times. I have never been fortunate enough to have seen a ghostly soldier, but every time I have

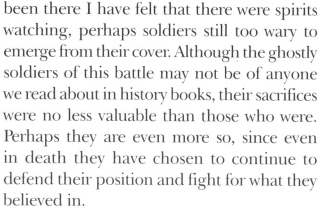

been there I have felt that there were spirits watching, perhaps soldiers still too wary to emerge from their cover. Although the ghostly soldiers of this battle may not be of anyone we read about in history books, their sacrifices were no less valuable than those who were. Perhaps they are even more so, since even in death they have chosen to continue to defend their position and fight for what they believed in.

One night, I did capture this photo when I turned quickly around after feeling a prickly feeling on the back of my neck, as if someone were watching me. When I took the photos to be developed, the woman that returned them to me asked me about this particular one and what it was. I replied that I did not know, but it was taken at the site of one of the largest battles in the Revolutionary War. "Do you think it could be a ghost?" she asked me. "I'd like to think so," I replied.

Orb at the Birmingham-Lafayette Cemetery.

Still on Duty

A Private Home in Concord Township

Lois loved Boston Terriers. She had a male Boston and when he was a couple of years old she had the opportunity to consider adding a female Boston to her household. In love with the idea of being surrounded by litters of her favorite dogs and being able to help other people by supplying the most adorable creatures in the world—more Boston Terriers—Lois adopted the female dog and brought her home. Right away, she discovered that she needed more room.

She was living in a two-bedroom apartment in Concord Township at the time and there was no real yard for the dogs to run around in. She decided to begin looking for a larger single house in the area, but they were all out of her price range.

"What am I going to do?" she would moan to me on the phone, "I have to find a bigger place." I suggested she ask her mother, who lived alone, to see if maybe she might be able to move in with her. If they put both of their assets and incomes together, they could probably afford a decent place. Although she was resistant at first, as weeks turned into months, she gave in. Her mother, of course, was thrilled at the prospect of having a new roommate, even if it was her daughter. Amazingly, within a few days of looking, her mother found a very nice, affordable home for them to buy. It was a small house, but it had two bedrooms and a big yard for the dogs.

Shortly after she moved in, she called me, very upset. "I think this was a mistake," she said.

"Oh, Lois, you and your mother will work things out. You have to give it a chance. It has to be better than that little apartment with no yard."

"It's not my mother," she said, "Mom's been surprisingly easygoing. It's the dogs!"

"Your mom knew about the dogs, though…" I started.

"No! My mom loves the dogs. The dogs hate the yard. They won't go out there. I could just cry. I have to take them into the front yard and all the neighbors look at me like I've lost my mind. I can't afford to move again and the reason I moved into this house was the yard! What am I going to do?!"

I was confused. "What do you mean the dogs won't go in the yard?" I asked her.

"They won't go!" She was almost crying. "I have to push them out the door and then hurry up and slam it before they get past me and back in. Then they carry on so bad and won't do their business that I have to let them back in, and then they started going in the house. So now I have to take them out front."

This was weird. My first thought was that there was some kind of wild animal nearby that was scaring them or leaving its scent in the yard. But when I asked her about that, she told me that she'd looked around and there were no woods or anything. And none of the neighbors seemed to have seen any large wild animals, either. We talked for a while longer and she seemed to calm down a little. So we ended the conversation with the hope that it was just an adjustment problem and the dogs would get over it.

They didn't get over it. The next time I talked to Lois, she advised that the dogs were still refusing to go in the yard and they would start shaking when she tried to put them there. I asked her if they did this at any other time or anywhere else.

They didn't. I was beginning to wonder if the dogs could see something in the yard that she couldn't—but I didn't want to scare her. I decided to just go over and visit her to see if there was a supernatural, rather than natural, explanation for her problem.

A Back Yard Visitor

When I got there, she welcomed me in and I could see that she and her mother had spent a lot effort to make the house their home. Both dogs were all over me from the minute I walked in the door. I couldn't believe they would cause any problems.

Lois offered to make some tea, and when we both had our steaming mugs, I asked if I could see the troublesome back yard.

"Sure! Why not? Just don't expect those two to come with us!" she said, pointing at the two terriers, which were curled up on the rug together.

When we exited the back door, I saw a nice, typical suburban sunny backyard. There were some lawn chairs sitting out, so we sat down with our tea and started to chat about various things—nothing too deep—and then I noticed it.

There was some kind of shadow at the back of the yard. When it first caught my eye, I thought it was just a shadow of a branch moving, but something about it wasn't right. I began to actively watch it and saw that the shadow moved back and forth in a straight line across the back of her yard. Lois noticed that I had gone quiet and asked what was wrong.

"Nothing," I replied, still watching the shadow.

"You see something don't you?" she asked excitedly. "I can tell you do."

All of my friends know that I study ghosts and the paranormal. They also know that I am sensitive to spirit presences and can often see and hear things of the spirit world that others can't.

"I'm not sure," I answered, "Let me take a closer look."

I walked towards the area where I saw the moving shadow. It wasn't moving anymore, so I had to look for a few minutes before I saw it, next to a tree. Then the outline of the shadow became clearer and I could see that it was not much taller than me, and appeared to be carrying something long across its front. The stance that it took reminded me of a police officer or guard challenging me as I entered a secure area.

"Are you a guard?" I asked the shadow.

When I said that I suddenly got a clear picture in my mind of what appeared to be a colonial soldier. He seemed very young and was wearing a sort of baggy shirt and tight pants. I couldn't see anything below his knees, but what he was holding seemed like a long gun. The shirt seemed darker than his trousers and he was wearing a dark hat that was rounded at the top. I was really shocked because I think of Colonial soldiers as looking like George Washington as he appeared on his horse—with a sword and everything. This guy didn't even resemble that at all!

Still, the message I was getting was that he was an American, not a British or Hessian soldier. His job, as I saw it, was to stay in that area and watch to see if any British troops came down the road.

Okay, I thought, *he must be talking about the main road down the hill a ways.* You couldn't see it now, but if the houses weren't there, it would have been visible.

But I still didn't understand why the dogs were so scared. I tried asking him about it, and I didn't really get much. I told him that Lois and her mother lived there and the dogs were their pets. Therefore, he was not to frighten them anymore. I told him the dogs were there to help protect the house, and that we understood that he was just doing his job, but the war ended over 200 years ago. We'd won our independence, so he was free to leave.

Oddly, he seemed to fade a little when I said that and then came back strongly with something like he had orders to stay until he was relieved or his commander gave him permission. He seemed unconcerned or unable to understand that a long period of time had passed. I figured that I would let it go at that and go tell Lois what I found.

She was not completely surprised, because she never really felt comfortable back there, either. Her mother had wanted to put a garden in and she kept putting it off because she didn't want to have to work in the back yard. I told her what was said and suggested that when she is going to let the dogs out, she should open the door and say something like, "I am letting my dogs out now. They need to be outside for a while," and see if that helped.

Things did calm down after that. The dogs would go in the yard, but she said they wouldn't stay there, and she never did feel comfortable enough to plant a garden in that space.

I asked one of my friends who was a re-enactor about the clothing I saw the ghost wearing, since it was so different from what I pictured a Colonial American soldier wearing. He said that, from my description, the ghost was probably from a militia of Maryland or Delaware. They often had to supply their own clothing, so his shirt would have been long and probably light brown. He also said that they wore rounded hats that turned up on one side like I'd described. The gun was also probably his own. My friend also said that even though it was tempting to associate the soldier with the battle of Brandywine, this was not necessarily true. He could have been from any time before the battle as well, as there were maneuvers going on all over southern Pennsylvania during the time leading up to the battle.

His suggestion for getting the ghost to leave his post was a good one—and one I hadn't thought of. He suggested we get a re-enactor from that militia unit to come and relieve him!

Chapter 5

The Chadds Ford Inn

Routes 1 & 100 in Chadds Ford, Pennsylvania

This historic building has undergone a lot of changes recently. First of all, it is not called the Chadds Ford Inn anymore, but the Brandywine Prime Seafood and Chops at the Chadds Ford Inn. It has been completely renovated, but the

The Chadds Ford Inn

[23]

main part of the building, from the outside at least, still looks the same. The inside is now opened up and modernized.

Although I am glad to see the place reopened and reinvented, I can't help but wonder if any of the history has been left intact. Most of all, what happened to the ghosts?

According to the old Chadds Ford Inn website, the inn started out as a family home of the Chads family. The records from the Chadds Ford Historical Society are not as clear on this point. It was stated that the building was converted from a home to an inn in 1736. The Historical Society records state that John applied for a tavern license in that year, but it is unclear within which building the tavern was located. The license states that it was to be in the home where he lived.

There is a John Chads house in Chadds Ford where it is known that he and his family lived. However, it does *look* like a house and I agree with the historical society in doubting whether this building was ever used as a tavern. It is possible that the tavern was operated at the building we know as the Chadds Ford Inn. John did own a large piece of land in that area.

The former owners of the Chadds Ford Inn claimed on their website that when he died in 1760, the inn was taken over by his nephew, Joseph Davis, and that it was during this time that the Chadds Ford Inn hosted some historic notables. Martha Washington stopped here on her way to visit her husband, George, at Valley Forge. General Lafayette also stopped here during his return trip to the Brandywine battleground.

During the Revolutionary War, the British soldiers raided the inn as well as most of the other homes and businesses in the area. They "commandeered" or stole all of the food and supplies. They also burned or otherwise destroyed the furnishings. Tax records from that time prove that the Inn sustained so much damage that no taxes were due on it, the livestock, or even the land. Both of these claims, if true, indicate that the owners of the Inn at the time must have been known patriots. Those loyal to the Crown rarely had their property completely destroyed.

Until the renovations and additions, the appearance of the inn was largely the same as it was in the days of Joseph Davis, The former owners boasted of having letters and a guest book from the 1700s on display. (I hope that these artifacts are safe somewhere!)

So What About the Ghosts?

The inn used to have a number of ghosts, including a little boy called Simon who mainly stayed on the second floor. There was also the spirit of a little girl named Katie. Most interesting, there was said to be the ghost of a sea captain who was spotted looking out the second floor windows. I have often wondered if he was a ferry captain or ferryman rather than a sea captain, since John Chads reason for licensing a tavern was to offer service for travelers who used his ferry service to cross the Brandywine.

During the former owner's tenure, water faucets turned off and on of their own accord, glasses moved across tables and crashed to the floor, lights flickered and dimmed, and doors were known to suddenly slam shut without the aid of human hands. What do these active and visible spirits think of the remodeling and changes?

According to an interview by Patricia Talarico with the new general manager, visitors ask about the ghosts. He says he has never seen anything to indicate the place was haunted, other than the lights sometimes getting suddenly brighter on their own—as if someone has accidentally hit a switch. *Hmmm.* It could be the same ghosts that liked to dim the lights before, when the inn was going downhill. Perhaps the brightening of the lights is their signal that they approve, and brighter days are coming for the historic property.

Author Snippet!

Visit another nearby restaurant with a reputation for being haunted! Pace One restaurant in Thornton, which used to be a barn, is located on Thornton Road, right down the road from the haunted barn in Chapter 15, featured in this book. The staff here has reported seeing the ghost of a man in various places in the building, mostly on the upper floors. He is believed to be the spirit of a man who lived there in the early 1900s and committed suicide on one of the upper floors. I didn't see him when I visited the restaurant, but maybe you will be more fortunate and catch a glimpse of this sad spirit.

Chapter 6

Haunted Bed and Breakfasts

There are a number of reportedly haunted inns and B&Bs in the Brandywine Valley area. Though quite a few of them have a reputation for having ghostly inhabitants, I always take the haunted inn stories with a grain of salt. You might be aware that, generally speaking, ghosts are good for business. Some haunted rooms in places like the Logan Inn in New Hope and B&Bs in Cape May have their haunted rooms booked solid for months in advance. Oddly, that is not the case with the inns of the Brandywine Valley. The proprietors here tend to either deny outright or downplay any ghost stories associated with their businesses, yet any internet search or chat with a local history buff will reveal the same stories cropping up again and again. If you are like me and believe that there is no smoke without fire, you might want to stay at one of these locations to see for yourself whether the ghost stories are true.

The Kennett House Bed and Breakfast (Formerly the Scarlett House)

Kennett Square, Pennsylvania

This house is built on property that was part of the original land grants given by William Penn to the Scarlett family. The house sits on a hill that is referred to as "Hessian Hill" because it was occupied by Hessian soldiers who were sent as reinforcements to assist the British in the Battle of Brandywine. The innkeepers deny experiencing any ghostly activity, but some former owners told stories of one room in particular where guests would report feeling a presence. This presence was never threatening and only made itself known to female guests. Perhaps it is a lonely male ghost looking for female companionship? It is not known who the ghost is or what its origins are. Maybe a former guest enjoyed his stay so much he decided to spend the afterlife there...

Hamanassett Bed and Breakfast

Chester Heights, Pennsylvania

Hamanassett was originally designed, in 1856, to be a retreat for physicians and residence for the owner. Unfortunately, the owner did not live to see his dream realized and the property was purchased by the Dohan family, who lived there for 130 years. It has been a Bed & Breakfast since 1984.

As with the Kennett House, the owners downplay any spirit activity. Again, guests that have stayed there have reported feeling a presence in one particular room in the main house. The presence was always described as peaceful, and some more sensitive guests have associated the presence with a female energy. There has been no history of tragedy associated with the house, so likely the female spirit there has just decided to stay on in a place where she was happy during her life, infusing the room she favors with her peaceful energy.

For more information, please visit their web site at
www.hamanassett.com.

Sweetwater Farm Bed and Breakfast

Glenn Mills, Pennsylvania

This posh inn is located on property that was part of a William Penn land grant to the Hemphill family. The oldest part of the inn was built in 1734. A more formal wing was added in 1815, but ghostly phenomena has been experienced in the older section of the inn. Once again, guests that have occupied the same room but are unknown to each other have reported the same thing. While they are asleep, their blankets are pulled from their bed. Legend links the ghost of this inn to a time in the house's history when it may have been part of the Underground Railroad, but since the experiences have all been in one of the upper floor rooms, I think this is a highly unlikely source for the haunting. It would have been very risky to keep runaway slaves in the upper rooms of a home where they would have to be smuggled up and down staircases and would have been trapped on upper floors if someone came looking for them. The blanket-pulling sounds to me like someone saying to the sleeping guests, "Hey! Get up and get out of my bed!" I think the ghost must be someone that once lived there and is very protective of their space.

For more information, visit their web site at
www.sweetwaterfarmbb.com.

Chapter 7

Disturbed by Spirits

A Private Home in Concord, Pennsylvania—near Route 202 and Smithbridge Road

I was sitting at the kitchen table at Parastudy (see Chapter 10) on one of our *Open House Psychic Reading* nights when a small group of young people came in. They were all in their late teens and early twenties and looked a little unsure of themselves. The hostess asked them if they wanted to sign up for a reading.

"Uh..., no," said one of the girls haltingly. "We really wanted to know if someone could help us. We think our house is haunted."

I immediately perked up. "What makes you think it's haunted?" I asked her.

"Different things keep happening. We are all afraid to be alone in the house. Our computers turn on when we aren't home. Radios turn on by themselves. Now this slimy stuff has started appearing on the hallway wall."

I was thinking it sounded a little *Amityville* to me, but they seemed sincere enough. They did look upset, so I knew that even if there was no ghost at their house, something had scared them. I offered to go over to the house and see what was going on.

"Can you come over right now?" they asked.

I wasn't expecting that, but if I could find a companion to accompany me, I was willing to go. One of the guys from

[30]

Parastudy offered to go along with me, so off we went, following them down Smithbridge Rd.

The house was pretty modern looking from the front. It didn't stand out at all among the other homes on the street. There was a sunroom in the rear and a pool in the backyard. I had my doubts, but I wasn't leaving without seeing the slime, so we went in.

I asked them not to tell me anything else about the structure or what happened there because I didn't want any preconceptions to interfere with my perceptions of the house and any possible spirits. As I stepped into the home, I saw that it looked like a typical house rented by a bunch of college students. There were lots of books, papers, shoes, coats, dishes, etc., on all the furniture and tables. I was drawn to the hallway.

"What's down here?" I asked.

"Oh, that's the bedrooms," answered the girl who had done all the talking at Parastudy.

"Can I go inside any of them?"

"Sure," she said, approaching me to follow behind.

We went down the hallway and I stopped in front of a door on my left. Unbelievably, unmistakably, there was a presence in this room! I glanced up at the ceiling and saw some kind of liquid dripping down the wall.

"Is this the slime?" I asked.

"Yes," she said, "It always appears on this wall right next to this room."

Unbelievable as it seemed, it did look like a slimy liquid. I touched the wet part of the wall. It also felt like a slimy liquid. I wasn't sure what connection this had, if any, with a ghostly presence, but there was one way to find out. I had to go into the room.

Upon entering, I was struck by how small it was. "The girl who stays in this room isn't here. She went back home for a few days," she offered.

Chapter 7

I walked around the space and then sat down on the bed. I had an overwhelming urge to cry. Whatever the spirit of this room was, it was not happy. The feeling was one of complete sadness. I told the residents that I needed a few minutes alone in the room to try and figure out what was going on. As I concentrated on the spirit, I got an impression of a young woman who lived in this area. The room seemed a bit *off* to me, but this was the area she stayed in. She was sad because she missed her family and she also indicated that she did not approve of many of the things that were going on in the house. Apparently, the spirit's religious beliefs included all forms of abstinence, including alcohol. She was upset by the amount of alcohol consumed in the house, especially that which was drunk by the ladies. She said that a Bible had been removed from the house and that the music that was played there was not Godly.

I tired to concentrate on her and a possible connection to the hallway slime, but there was nothing there. Perhaps another ghost? We would see. In the meantime, I felt that she would be soothed by the presence of a Bible in the room. She would also be more content if they could place some religious music, like hymns.

I wasn't sure if the current residents would be obliging, but I went out to tell them what I had learned so far. They were shocked. The Bible had been in the house when they moved in—in the top of the closet in that room. Since they weren't really religious, they had just donated it with a bunch of other stuff they didn't want any more. They said it wasn't a really old Bible or anything, and they had totally forgotten about it until I mentioned it.

As for the alcohol consumption, they all started laughing. Imagine, a house full of college students that drink a *little*. They did say that they didn't think their drinking was excessive, but sometimes they did drink too much. The girls said that drinks were often moved from where they thought they left them and bottles of beer had come up missing, which had been a source of many arguments in the house. They were now thinking that maybe their ghost was to blame for these incidents. It is possible that the ghost had a hand in it, but that was something that could never be proven. I said that they might be able to reach a compromise with the ghost if they would try to drink outside the house.

We came up with another compromise for the religious music. They said they would be happy to leave a radio or the TV on a religious music station while they were away from the house. I encouraged them to tell her what they were doing while they were doing it, such as, "We are leaving now, so we are going to put on the music that you like." I was waiting for someone to ask me if I could make her leave, but they didn't, so I left it at that.

Something Is Not Right...

As we walked down to the end of the hallway and the last bedroom, I asked them if the house was changed or moved. I mentioned that when I was in the room alone it seemed a bit *off*, as if the placement was not quite right. They responded that they didn't know, but one of the girls offered us an experience that she had one night in the dining room that may have related to this.

She was sitting at the table working on a paper. She looked up as she was thinking about something and she saw movement outside the window. It seemed blurry and out of focus at first, but then gradually came into focus. What she saw was a woman in old-fashioned clothes, standing at some kind of sink washing dishes. This was outside the window, not inside the house. The strange thing was, it was as if the girl was looking into a room that wasn't there anymore. As she watched, it faded away and was gone.

Until I had mentioned that the rooms may have been moved, she had just written it off as imagination. They didn't know any of the history of the house. The only thing that may account for this is that there may have been an older house on the lot that was demolished before this one was built.

The last room was the largest room and was shared by two of the girls. They informed me that this was the room where the computers went crazy all the time and the TV acted up, turning off and on and changing channels by itself. They also said that the clock radios were very undependable, with the alarm turning off, resulting in their oversleeping.

I walked around the room, trying to pick up on something that could be a source of disturbance. I wasn't getting anything. I sat for a while alone and then with the girls who stayed in that room. Still I was getting nothing. It was clear that they were disappointed and really hoped that this upsetting problem could be solved. Finally, my escort from Parastudy came up with an idea. "Why don't we just walk around the outside of the house?"

"Okay," I said, "Let's go." At this point we weren't getting anything inside, so why not? As we walked around outside we stopped periodically to take pictures and EMF readings. EMF stands for electro magnetic field. Electromagnetic fields are found just about everywhere. When we first go to a haunted location, we like to get a baseline reading of the electromagnetic fields—identifying things that can make the EMF meter spike such as transformers, electrical boxes, household appliances, outlets, etc. Once the base readings are acquired, fluctuations or changes can be compared to or noted from the baseline reading. These changes can be caused by contact with an EMF from a normal source or a paranormal source. If the change is caused by something paranormal, it will fluctuate or give a completely abnormal reading and then go back to normal or baseline.

When we came around the corner of the room where the electrical disturbances happened, we noticed a jump on the EMF meter. In looking around, all we could see was that all of the wires were coming into the house at that point—wires for electric, cable, phone, etc. We followed the lines away from the house to see where they met with the pole. It was down at the street level, which was not close enough to cause the jump in EMF, especially since we saw that the meter didn't move when we got closer to the pole.

As we went back toward the house, the same jump in EMF happened in a different spot as we got closer to the outside wall of the bedroom. I began taking photos of the outside of the house. Orbs showed up in almost every picture of that side of the house. As I walked back towards the other side, where one girl said she had a vision of another room outside, our EMF stayed level and we got no orb photos.

We walked back towards the other side of the house and began to get orb photos again. Clearly there was something going on at this side of the house. I wasn't sure what it was because all I could pick up psychically was an uncomfortable feeling of being watched, as if someone was going to come around the side of the house any second and yell, "Boo!"

Some theories about ghosts and how they are able to manifest hold that they are able to make use of existing electromagnetic energy in order to appear and/or effect our physical environment. This is why electrical appliances or equipment may stop working in the presence of a spirit, or new batteries may be drained. People who are sensitive will also often feel literally drained of energy in the presence of spirits. In the case of this house, I felt we had an opportunistic spirit who was able to use the higher level of electricity at that point, as well as the higher number of electronic gadgets in that room to his advantage. Yes, I said *his* because the energy that I was feeling there was definitely malc.

I encouraged them to try to get the cable wire moved or ask the landlord about having the entry spot rewired to eliminate any possible problems from older or partially exposed wires.

As we left that evening, they said they would check on the history of the property and I assured them that I would be in touch to see how things were working out. I e-mailed them a week later and they advised that the slimy stuff was gone. We never did make an association for a spirit with that. To this day, I have no idea what that was or what caused it and have never seen anything like that since.

About a month later, I e-mailed them again and got no response. When I called, the number was out of service. The next chance I had, I drove by the house to see if they were still there. The house was empty and there was a "For Rent" sign in the window. I never heard from any of them again, but I have often wondered about the spirits in the house. I drive by there every so often and have noticed that the "For Rent" sign appears in that window very frequently. I guess the ghost inhabitants are still there...

Chapter 8

Colonial Pennsylvania Plantation

Ridley Creek State Park, Media, Pennsylvania

One hears conflicting reports about whether this place is haunted or not. I can say, after having visited it, that it is most definitely haunted! Personally, I'd always heard rumors about the place being haunted, but the rumors always lacked specifics. The plantation was included on a local radio station's

The Plantation House.

Halloween tour of genuinely haunted places, so I always thought there must be something there.

Ever the ghost hunter, when I heard my daughter's class trip was to the Colonial Pennsylvania Plantation, I gave her a disposable camera and said, "Take a picture anywhere you feel like there might be a ghost." When she returned with a used-up camera, I asked her, "Well, how was it?" She replied, "Well, there was really only one room that I felt funny in. That was where they did the spinning. They used me as a model, so I asked my teacher to take pictures."

When the photos came back, I found that she had taken many photos of the inside of the plantation as well as some of her and her friends at lunch. Every photo of the room where the spinning demonstration was conducted had small circular "orbs." None of the other pictures had orbs in them. Although this in itself is not proof of a paranormal presence, it piqued my interest about the possibility of a ghost at the plantation.

At Halloween, the plantation offered an event where ghost stories were told. I was unable to attend that date, so I made a phone call to the office and asked if there was anyone I could speak to about the ghost stories. "Oh," said the voice on the other end of the line, "all of the ghost stories are made up. They aren't things that really happened."

"So the Plantation is *not* haunted?" I asked. "No," replied the woman, but with a hesitation in her voice. I didn't hang up; I just waited for her to work up the courage…And she said, "Well, the house probably is haunted. I mean, it is very old."

"Okay," I said, "Would I be able to speak with anyone about why you think it is probably haunted?" Unfortunately, she wasn't that brave. "No," she said, "There isn't anyone who can talk to you about that."

Never one to be put off, I visited the Colonial Plantation during their Wassail Tour. The volunteer guides denied experiencing anything ghostly, but did admit that the house has a reputation for being haunted.

As we toured the house with the extremely knowledgeable and helpful guides, I didn't feel anything out of the ordinary. Then we entered the room where they do the spinning. *Wow!* I thought, and whispered to my companion, "There is someone here."

The presence of a woman was very, very strong. I had to be silent for a moment and try and get a feel for what was there.

Spinning Out of Control

The guide offered to do some spinning for us, and sat down to prepare. She began showing us the wool, which she explained came from the sheep that live there. She showed us the parts of the spinning wheel and told how they had to make all their own clothing in colonial times. Continuing with her set up, she began to dig through the pile of wool.

"Well, that's odd," she said, "I know I put one in here."

"What?" I asked.

"A hook," she answered. "It is much easier to get it threaded with the hook."

She then continued to dig through the second basket of wool, looking for the hook. She actually got up off the seat and dumped all the wool into one basket and then really looked through the wool.

No hook.

"I guess I will have to get one from the weaver," she said, "but I know I had one there this morning." She left the room with a puzzled look on her face.

"Hmmm," I thought to myself, "Objects that disappear from places you know you put them…" She came back with a hook and the rest of the demonstration was uneventful.

Then we entered the weaving room. The guide explained the weaving process in great detail, demonstrating all of the various steps and tools used in the process of weaving linen and linsey-woolsey. As I stood with my back to the flax pounder, I felt a child's hand push its way into my right pocket and into my right hand, just as a young person would. It took about a second for me to realize that there were no children with us, and another second to whisper to my companion, "Trade places with me." I was a little unnerved by the experience to stay there, but I didn't want to appear rude and just walk out during the demonstration. Besides, I wanted to see if the child would follow me or pick someone else.

A few seconds after I had moved, the man who had been standing to my right, where the hand emerged from, also asked his companion to trade places with him. He didn't say why. Did he feel a small hand in his pocket or on his sleeve? Or did he just get that uncomfortable feeling that accompanies sharing space with a ghost? He didn't say.

Who is the child in the weaving room? The hand emerged from the area of the flax pounder, a job which was often given to children, according to the guide. Could this child still be doing his chores? I say "his" because the impression that I got of this child was of a young boy, possibly four or five years old.

Another fact to take note of is that the weaving room is believed to be the oldest building on the property, according to Colonial Plantation literature, "but its exact age and original use are uncertain." The guide that we spoke to told us that they believe it was the first dwelling built on the property,

Spinning wheel with the basket
from which the hook disappeared.

and was used by the original owner until the main house was built. Plantation literature reports that, "archaeological evidence indicates that in more recent years it has been used for smoking meats and storage."

The families that lived here, the Lewis's and then the Pratts, were Quakers. They typically had large families, including about

six children and a number of extended family members, such as aunts or grandparents. Their household likely included a number of servants.

As for the identity of the spirits that I encountered there, I believe they once resided there. For colonial families, the home was the center of their lives. Quaker children and women rarely left home except to go to weekly Meeting. In the eighteenth and nineteenth century, it was so common for children to pass away from various illnesses and accidents. There is no record of the death of a woman or a child on the property; however, we must remember that until very recently most people were born, lived, and then died at their home.

Chapter 3

Cursed Ground

A Cul-de-Sac in Thornbury Township

"There are places in the earth where foul deeds have ripped a gaping maw to the very world of the dead, and unseemly things have escaped from nighted pits. Such places are cursed; blasted barren landscapes where no sane man should go."
S. M. Arthweight, *Cursed Places—a Tome of Sorrows 1873*

Many students of the occult and the paranormal are familiar with the seemingly cursed town of Dudleytown, Connecticut. The legend of the curse of Dudleytown grew from the disproportionate number of early and accidental deaths that befell the settlers, as well as an unusually high incidence of insanity among the residents. Is this the result of a curse or coincidence? A similar situation and question confronted the residents of a cul-de-sac in Thornbury Township.

"The concept of synchronicity indicates a meaningful coincidence of two or more events, where something other than the probability of chance is involved. Chance is a statistical concept which 'explains' deviations within certain patterns of probability. Synchronicity elucidates meaningful arrangements and coincidence which somehow go beyond the calculations of probability. There are phenomena which are inexplicable through chance, but become empirically intelligible through the

employment of the principle of synchronicity, which suggests a kind of harmony at work in the interrelation of both psychic and physical events."

—Carl G. Jung from, *Synchronicity: An Acausal Connecting Principle*

Thornbury Township, like much of southeastern Pennsylvania, was once the home of the Lenni-Lenape Indians. Not much is known of what may have happened here in pre-colonial days. The land within the present boundaries of Thornbury Township was taken up by "first purchasers" from William Penn.

The Battle of the Brandywine, the only major battle of the Revolution fought in Pennsylvania, was within sight and sound of the western part of the Township; at that time approximately three hundred people lived in there. In its early history, Thornbury Township was part of Chester County. In forming Delaware County, Thornbury Township was divided. People who owned property near the border were asked whether they wished to live in Chester County or Delaware County. This is the reason for the jagged shape of the present boundary.

Today, Thornbury Township is a quiet place. This former rural area of open fields and forest areas are being cleared for development. Some of these areas have never been inhabited by more than trees or farm crops. In one pastoral area, when people moved in to their new homes, a series of misfortunes began. It started when a young person in his teens died in a car accident. A short time later, another young man on the same street died in a similar accident. Then two people in two separate homes were diagnosed with cancer. One of the residents died. The other went into remission and moved away. After that, another young person died an accidental death under mysterious circumstances. Not that strange, right?

Well it is when you consider that this all happened in less than ten years in one cul-de-sac on Magnolia Lane. This cul-de-sac has only five homes on it.

That wasn't all. One of the women who lost her son to a car accident, lost her mother *and* her husband within a year. Her husband died of complications resulting from MS. He had been diagnosed shortly after moving to Magnolia Lane.

A House With a History

All of this information was related to me by a woman named Patricia, one of the prior residents of this cul-de-sac. She had since moved, but was feeling remorseful about not sharing her idea regarding the possible curse with the new owners of her former home. When I asked her why she felt there was a curse, she replied that she was unsure, but had always felt like something was hanging over that neighborhood. Then there were the flies. She said, hesitating, "We also had a weird problem with flies in our bedroom...circling above the bed."

At this point, I was wondering what the various causes of this negativity could be. When I asked her if she had remained in contact with the people she sold the house to, she said she had. The new owners had been so disturbed by some of the things that happened in the house that they had called her.

"They told my daughter and I that when the wife was alone in the house and was getting ready for a wedding, she'd laid out her newly dry-cleaned clothes on the bed and got into the shower. When she returned to the bedroom she found her clothes were thrown all over the room. She was so unnerved by the experience that they moved out of the house soon after. They then rented the house to some students."

The owner was unable to keep tenants in the house and had to move back into it. About a year later, he again contacted Patricia because he wanted to sell the house and his family had been experiencing some very unusual things again. His step-children reported seeing a young man in one of the bedrooms. They believed that this was Patricia's son, who was one of the young men who had died in a car accident. They also called in a medium to try and figure out the nature of the phenomena they were experiencing.

Patricia, understandably upset, called me and told me what was happening. I discouraged her from assuming it was her son's spirit, reminding her of what she had told me regarding her feelings that the property was somehow cursed. If it really was cursed, then it was possible that an entity associated with the negative energy of the curse saw an opportunity to bring her back into its realm of influence.

Against my advice and her own intuition, she visited her former home. She called me the next day, extremely upset and shaken. "I need to talk to you...Something very messed up happened after I went to my old house."

She told me that she took a bottle of holy water with her. She had gone into the bedroom where they claimed to have seen her son, and sprinkled the water all over the place. The new owners told her all about the medium and what he'd said. Of course, the medium claimed the spirit was her son. The whole experience had been recorded and they offered her a DVD so she could see for herself what was said while the medium was there. They told her that he was returning for further investigation and would like her to be there as well. She said she'd agreed, adding that she would like to meet him.

As soon she got into her car, she began to shake and was overcome with a feeling of dread. She didn't know why she'd said she wanted to meet the medium. She didn't believe the spirit was her son. She didn't believe in consulting mediums to speak with the deceased. That was against everything she believed in. What had she been thinking? She had to get away from there. As she started driving, she noticed the DVD lying on the seat next to her. She grabbed it and threw it out the window, afraid of what it contained.

"Would you believe I almost got sucked in?" she asked. I explained to her that is how those things happen. When an evil entity has you under its influence, it does not want to let you get away. She was horrified that in the brief time she was in the house, she began to think a medium was not so bad, and yes, she would like to meet him.

Later that night, her younger daughter was relating the events to her sister, who lives away from home. As she got to the part about the holy water, her daughters both heard a loud voice on the line. "She did it!" the voice growled. Her daughter dropped the phone in terror and ran to tell her mother what had happened. She believes this voice was the spirit from Magnolia Lane, angry about the holy water. She decided to turn away from the past completely and swore to never return, but it is not easy for her.

Shortly after that night, Patricia was contacted by the family about returning to meet with the medium. She refused, stating that it was against her beliefs and she wanted to distance herself from the events on Magnolia Lane. Unbelievably, the medium sent her a nasty e-mail asking her, "How could you, as a mother, leave your son's soul there to be lost? What kind of mother are you?" This really upset her, but I assured her that this is how these evil entities work and I encouraged her to stick with what she believed was right. These things play upon your fears and weaknesses to try and get you to doubt your beliefs. She mustered all her strength and faith to reply to the medium. She said, "Whatever is there is not my son. I know my son is in heaven."

She said that he e-mailed her back, but she did not read it. That is probably the best thing she could have done. She asked me if the curse will ever leave her alone. I had to tell her the truth—I didn't know. As I said, once an evil entity had you in its circle of influence, it doesn't like to lose you.

A curse, according to Merriam-Webster, is "a prayer or invocation for harm or injury to come upon one," or "an evil or misfortune that comes as if in response to imprecation."

Curses are cast to exact revenge or to protect against the violation of homes, treasures, and gravesites, as well as to punish those who stole or moved sacred objects. Egyptians, for instance, employed curses to protect their final resting places on Earth, since they believed that the conditions of these places had a direct influence on the afterlife. Could this land have once been sacred? Could it have been a burial ground? Very little information is available concerning the history of this land as it has been undeveloped and used as pasture land for centuries.

Chapter 10

Parastudy

Valleybrook Road—Chester Heights, Pennsylvania

The Haunts at www.parastudy.com

With a name like 'Parastudy' it would have to be haunted, right?

Parastudy is an organization that provides a setting and resources to help people in their "unrestricted search for enlightenment." It hosts lectures and classes on any number of new age subjects, such as Reiki, Feng Shui, UFOs, the Unexplained, and more. They host monthly psychic reading nights to help raise money for their non-profit organization and even have a new age book store with a wide range of books and supplies to help visitors and members in their quest for enlightenment.

I was first introduced to Parastudy when I was still in high school by a friend of mine whose mother was a member. My first visit was during their annual "Come As You Were" Halloween party where guests were encouraged to dress as one of their past life personas. It was very interesting to see the range of costumes; there were soldiers, scribes, ancient Egyptians, and Victorians, as well as dancers, teachers, scholars, and mystics. The environment was liberating for someone like me who had grown up in a home where things like past lives and tarot cards were of "the devil."

Chapter 10

Every chance I had, I returned to Parastudy. It was one place where I could really ask questions about ghosts and spirit communication. In addition, I was finally getting encouragement to develop my own psychic abilities with lots of positive reinforcement and good advice. The only thing that I wasn't hearing about was my main interest, which was, of course, GHOSTS! It seemed as if no one at Parastudy was interested in ghosts at all. I would ask about ghosts and I would get the answer, "Well, you know, the house *is* haunted." I never got more than that and never heard anyone actually say they saw or experienced their resident ghost.

After a few years of moving around after high school, I found myself settled once again in Delaware County, Pennsylvania. One of the first things I did was check to see if Parastudy was still there, and happily, it was. When I returned to Parastudy, I saw the same faces and ran into the same wall. No one seemed interested in ghosts! When I asked, I received the same response as before, that the house was haunted. Then I saw that one of the listed discussion events in October that year was called "Ghosts."

Finally, I thought. *They will have to talk about the ghost, or at least about ghosts.* My excitement died as I arrived at Parastudy and it was soon clear that the only people attending this meeting would be me, my companion, and about three board members. The discussion mainly consisted of me relating my own ghost experiences to them! I realized that if I wanted to find the ghost, if there was one at Parastudy, I was on my own.

I went off to check out the front staircase again. Nothing. I felt nothing! I decided to stroll around the second floor and see if maybe there was something up there. There are several rooms upstairs at Parastudy, including an office, a meditation room, a library, and the New Age Book Store. None of these rooms set off anything in my senses. When I reached the end of the hallway, I noticed that there was another flight of stairs that led to the first floor. It was much narrower and steeper than

Parastudy's Victorian House.

the front staircase and had a low ceiling that gave it a boxed-in feel. As I went to take a step onto the first stair, all of my senses went off. There was no way I was going down those stairs.

Okay, I reasoned with myself, *You're alone in a dark, narrow staircase. You're just getting an attack of claustrophobia. There is nothing stopping you from just taking a quick walk down the stairs and back up again.* As I lifted my foot towards the top stair, I was once again met by an overwhelming feeling of dread coupled with the certainty that there was no way I was going to be able to descend those stairs. Maybe, at last, I had found a ghost at Parastudy!

I returned to the kitchen via the front staircase and inquired about the back stairs. "Oh yes," I was told, "those stairs lead down to the landing between the kitchen and the dining room. They are the old servant's stairs."

"Has anyone ever felt anything odd on the stairs? Or seen anything?" I asked.

"Like what?" they wanted to know.

I was intrigued. *They didn't immediately say no,* I thought to myself. "Like not wanting to, or not being able to, go down them," I said.

My excitement was short-lived. "Well, you know," one member started, and then finished with the *Parastudy Party Line*, "The house *is* haunted."

I could have screamed in frustration. I was still on my own.

I returned to the staircase and there was still that awful feeling of dread. I didn't see or hear anything, just felt it. I returned home that night, still frustrated at my inability to discover if that place was really haunted. I know that what I felt on the stairs was real, but what did it mean?

More determined than ever, I spent as much time as I could at Parastudy. I noticed that the back stairs were rarely, if ever, used. Members would take the long way around to the front stairs and then back to the kitchen. I don't know whether their avoidance of the stairs was unconscious or deliberate, but it was definitely interesting. Photos and recordings I took on the back stairs never yielded anything, but patience and perseverance is something that all paranormal investigators must have. A good deal of luck is often needed to capture photographic or recorded evidence of a spirit presence. One must be in the right place at the right time.

Possible corroboration of what I felt came during one of the picnics when a new member was taking some photos of the outside of the house. Since I was the "ghost person" at the time, she had been sent to ask me about one of the photos.

"Do you see anything in this photo?" she asked me.

I looked at it, searching for an orb or maybe a misty area. I didn't see anything.

"Look at this window," she said, and she began to zoom in with her LED display. The window she was looking at was the window in the room right at the top of the back stairs. I saw what she was excited about. In the window was what appeared to be a woman, looking out at us. There had been no one upstairs at the time. In fact, I was told by the office manager that since the picnic was going on, all the upstairs rooms were closed and locked.

While I was working on the back stairs ghost, I became involved in some fund-raising activities for Parastudy. We decided to have a garage sale to clear out some of the "junk" that had accumulated in the garage. A lot of the sorting and pricing of items fell to me, so I enlisted the help of one of my friends, Tara, to help me get ready for the sale.

We were inside the garage sorting and pricing books. The front doors were wide open because it was very warm that day. From where we stood, we had a clear view of the driveway approaching Parastudy. As we chatted and worked, people stopped by to drop off more donations and others stopped by to try to get a preview of the sale. At one point, I looked up and saw an older gentleman walk in the doors and disappear behind a large cabinet to our left.

"Tara," I whispered, "Did you see that guy?"

"Yes," she answered, "He went around the cabinet over there." She pointed to where I saw him go.

"Well, that's it!" I said, "He has to leave. We're never going to get this done if I have to keep stopping to chase away the early birds!"

I marched over to the side of the garage where the cabinet was. I knew I would have him cornered, because we had tables and cabinets blocking any access to the back of the garage. I rounded the corner to confront the man, took a deep breath, and held it. There was no one there.

"Tara!" I called out, "Is the man over there?"

"No," she called back, "How could he be over here? He went behind those cabinets!"

"Well," I said, "He's not here now!"

We both left the garage and stared at the open doors from the outside. We could see the whole interior now and there was no one there. Tara went inside the house to get someone else to check out the barn.

What the heck? I thought to myself. *The heat must be getting to us.*

She quickly returned with one of the maintenance volunteers. As he approached me he asked, "Did you see him leave?"

"No," I replied, "There's no one here. It's so strange because we both saw the same thing."

"What did he look like?" asked the volunteer.

"Well, he was old, had gray hair, and dressed like a farmer or like he was doing yard work," I said.

The man looked thoughtfully at us and said, "Well, I think you have seen a ghost."

"What?" I yelled. "No one ever told me there was a ghost out here!"

"Well, not many people have seen him, but there was a man who used to take care of everything out here. He took care of the yard and maintenance of this place up until he died. All this stuff that we are going through is stuff he collected. He used to have a yard sale every weekend."

Finally, there it was; luck! When I least expected it and when I didn't have a camera. At least I had a witness.

The sale went well and we didn't see the ghost again. One night, my husband and I were driving out that way and decided to stop in. Parastudy was closed, but I thought I would just take a few photos of the barn and the house to see what showed up. I walked around to the front of the house to get a photo of the Victorian building and heard the car start down the driveway. I quickly snapped a few photos and headed back to the car, assuming he was telling me to hurry up. When I opened the door he greeted me with, "Thank God it's you. This place gives me the creeps."

"Why?" I asked him.

"When I was parked back by the garage, I swear I could hear someone walking towards the car. When I looked up, thinking it was you, there was no one there."

I wondered whether I should tell him about the ghost of the caretaker that Tara and I saw a few years before. *No,* I thought to myself, *better tell him when it's daylight.* He is always good about accompanying me to haunted places, but he does not want to experience anything himself. Also, I knew if I told him right then, there was no way he was ever going to agree to come back to Parastudy with me, and it is definitely a place that warrants further investigation.

Chapter 11

Newlin Grist Mill

219 South Cheney Road, Glen Mills, Pennsylvania

I wasn't sure what to expect from the grist mill. It is certainly old enough to merit a haunting, but the reports of whether the mill is haunted or not and by whom are so varied that it is difficult to believe anything about it being haunted. Nevertheless, according to the park literature, it *is* the only functioning colonial grist mill in the United States and that alone should earn it a visit.

The mill is located on the corner of Cheney Road and Baltimore Pike, not far from the Brandywine Battlefield Park. According to their literature, the mill was built in 1704 by Nathaniel Newlin, whose father, Nicholas, had emigrated from Ireland after obtaining his land grant from William Penn in 1683. The mill was owned and operated by the Newlin family until 1817. The mill didn't stop operation until 1941.

I first read about ghosts at the Mill complex, which includes the Mill, the Miller's House, the Trimble House, a Springhouse, a Barn, and a Blacksmith's Shop, in the book, *In Search of Ghosts*, by Elizabeth P. Hoffman. In it, she recounts the story of a couple who lived in the miller's house (no dates) and saw and heard the ghost of a woman in their home. They eventually had a full séance to make contact with the spirit and, according to Hoffman, they all lived happily ever after.

After visiting and doing some research, I am unable to discover which house they were referring to in the story. The house that is now called The Miller's House was, as far as I can tell, always in use when it was occupied by a member of the Newlin family. The Trimbles did take over operation and ownership of the mill in 1817, but they had their own house, built in 1739, to the right and up the hill from the Miller's house. Park literature states that the Newlin family was actively involved in administration of the mill until 1941, when it closed.

Sarah's Plight

How then, and when, did this drama that created the pitiful ghost of Sara occur? According to Hoffman, the medium, speaking in the heavily-German accented voice of Sarah, told of being taken from the workhouse at age twelve to look after the home and sons of an abusive miller that lived in the miller's

The Miller's House today.

house at Newlin Mill. There is only one record of a Sarah marrying into the Newlin family, according to the genealogy on the Newlin Grist Mill website, but this marriage was in 1782, and her husband, Thomas Newlin, was a blacksmith, not a miller. There was a poorhouse on Cheney Road, which was located on the grounds of what is currently the Delaware County Jail, right up the road from the mill, so perhaps this is the workhouse she refers to. In any case, the spirit of Sarah went on to mention the Civil War, which places her life in the mid-nineteenth century. At that time, the Newlins were no longer millers, so it couldn't have been one of them anyway.

Could Sarah have lived in the Trimble House? Possibly, although doubtful. The Trimbles, like the Newlins, were Quakers, and I find it highly unlikely that, as the spirit of Sarah says, the Trimble sons were anxious to enlist and fight in the Civil War. Very few Quakers enlisted and fought in the war; they are almost always conscientious objectors. Sarah's story, although very interesting, doesn't have information to back it up. So, I must say that I doubt that the miller's house was haunted by a ghost named Sarah.

In Charles Adams' book, *Ghost Stories of Delaware County*, he revisits the story of the female ghost at the mill, interviewing a member of Parastudy who remembered when the woman who reported the ghost of Sarah was an active member of the group. She had been telling the members of all the ghostly events and sightings taking place there, stating that the family was renting the house in 1963. (Finally, a date!) The problem with this timeline is that during the 1960s, the house was owned and being renovated by Elizabeth Battles Newlin and her family. According to the park website, it was during the 1960s that the entire top floor of the house was removed and the house was renovated and furnished with the period furniture pieces that are on display there today. This doesn't sound like a rental property to me, but I suppose there is a small window of possibility.

This leaves us again at the Trimble House, the only other home on the property. This house, as far as I can tell, was never rented to anyone, but was always privately owned and is still privately owned today.

Haunted?

So, are any of the mill buildings haunted? Well, during my visit there I did feel rather uncomfortable in the old part of the mill. Since there was only one person working there in the office the day I visited, I was left alone to tour the mill at my leisure. I spent some time walking around the upstairs displays, learning the history of the mill and Concord Township as well. For some reason, I kept thinking of the name Clara.

I must admit at this point that this was not my first time considering the story of the mill. Remember, I was an active member of Parastudy for quite some time and had heard the story of the ghost at the mill a few times. Oddly, I would always get the name wrong when retelling it and refer to the ghost as Clara, not Sarah. So, is there a Clara in the Newlin family tree? Sadly, there is not, so the mystery of my association of the name Clara with the mill remains unsolved.

When I was upstairs, I thought I heard someone come in downstairs, so I went down to see if it was the tour guide, wondering what took me so long and whether I fell into the millworks or something. When I got to the bottom, I saw there was no one there. I looked outside and I could see that I was alone on that side of the park. As I walked past the mill, I got the sensation of someone staring at me from the windows. It was very unnerving, so I decided to take a picture.

That is the photo you see here of the mill. When I downloaded the photos at home and looked through them, my daughter looked over and said, "Who's that in the window?" I looked, and it does, indeed, look as if someone is staring out the window. The figure appears in the window on the second floor to the far right. It appears to me to have its arms folded and is wearing a white apron over the lower half of its body. I thought it looked like a man; my daughter thought it was a woman. I don't know. All I know is that I was sure someone was looking at me from the mill building.

A photo taken of the inside of the room at this window shows that there are no mannequins or figures in the room.

As I walked outside, trying to shake off the feeling of being watched, I took some photos of the Miller's House. As I did, the name Samuel kept coming to mind. I felt as if someone was telling me there was something important to do with someone named Samuel. Well, the guide advised that if I had any questions to come back to the office across the street and ask. So I did.

In response to my question about someone named Samuel being associated with the mill, he responded very positively, "Oh yes, Samuel Newlin Hill was the last owner of the mill when it closed in 1941. He and his brother had a big disagreement and closed the mill and sold it."

Was Samuel the one watching me from the window? I doubt that I will ever be able to know for sure. What I can say is that I do believe the mill is haunted, but it is not haunted in the active, poltergeist way described in the earliest account of the haunting. I feel that the spirit at the mill is one that just watches over it, protectively, making sure the mill remains the oldest functioning grist mill in the United States.

The Mill.

The interior of the Mill—second floor.

Chapter 12

The Crier in the Country

1 Crier in the Country Lane, Glen Mills, Pennsylvania

In Delaware County, there are always stories about this place or that place being haunted. Everyone seems to "know" that the Crier in the Country Restaurant is one of those places.

Exterior of the Crier.

Today, it even looks haunted. It sits, empty and forlorn, at the top of the hill. Its dark, empty windows face the traffic that flies by it on Route 1. Sadly, this once grand home and stately restaurant is slated for demolition as the building itself has become somewhat of a ghost of its former self.

The Crier changed hands at the beginning of 2007. It was purchased by a catering company that hopes to turn this historical site into a catering facility that would completely replace the current building, although they plan to incorporate some of the old fixtures into the new building. At the first zoning hearing for the planned changes, the new owner was reportedly told by the township, "You can't tear down the building. Lydia won't let you." Lydia is the spirit that everyone "knows" haunts the Crier.

After this meeting, I was contacted by the new owners. They heard that I was familiar with the paranormal residents of the property and wanted me to come out and make sure that the spirit inhabitants would accept their planned changes to the site. It seems that a bigger problem is the township's acceptance of the proposed changes. Almost eight months later, what's left of the building is still standing.

The last time I was there, I looked at the gouged hardwood floors and piles of ripped-out wood trim. Over all the devastation, the crystal chandelier still glowed and shone and the graceful staircase wound its way up to the second floor. Walking through piles of plaster rubble and past piles of furniture, I couldn't help but think back to the first time I visited the Crier, and how beautiful it had once been.

It was about ten years ago, and the restaurant had just been purchased by the Jackson Brothers. We visited the restaurant in search of a good place to hold the annual Y100 Halloween séance. I had suggested this restaurant because, like many of residents of Delaware County, I "knew" it was haunted.

When I was in high school, I worked part time as a page at the Ridley Township Public Library (part of which is haunted, but that is another tale). One of our jobs was to read the shelves. Reading the shelves meant we had to stand in front of a shelf of library books and read the catalogue numbers on the spines, making sure the books were in order and replacing those that were not. My favorite section to "read" was the one that contained our extremely limited collection of books on the paranormal. Often, I would pick up a volume and read the book rather than the shelf in front of me. It was in this manner that I read a copy of *The Ghostly Gazetteer* by Arthur Meyers. Entry number thirty-three was about the Crier in the Country, a restaurant that housed a spirit frightening enough to have scared a German Shepherd to death! Our radio show was intrigued, too, and since the owners were very hospitable and open to the possibility of their new restaurant being haunted, we decided to hold the séance there.

A Nasty Encounter

We were unable to make contact with the spirit of Lydia, but we did experience the nasty spirit on the third floor. As I entered the bedroom with two other psychics, I was flooded with images of a young girl, cowering on her bed, which was in the corner. A very large man was advancing towards her. The vision became too much for me, so I had to leave the room.

One of the radio show hosts talked me into going back up. The ghostly man was still there, challenging any of us to make him depart. I tried to let him know that we were not there to make him leave; we just wanted to bring him peace. He was resistant to all efforts to communicate. We were unsure why he chose to remain at the site of his apparent crime. Incidentally, there was no record of this crime to my knowledge. However, the vision I had was of the girl's body being buried secretly on the property, with her belongings. It seemed odd that the spirit of this young girl, who I saw being violated and murdered did not remain, seeking justice. It was clear, though, why no other spirit would choose to share this space with the spirit on the third floor. He was truly a repellant character.

More—or Less—Haunts!

On the first and second floors, the spirits are of a more gentle and of a genteel sort. The resident spirits are believed to be Lydia Pennel and Henry Saulnier, two people who owned and loved this home. At my initial visit, I encountered the spirit of a man with an injured leg by the front room fireplace. I saw him with a cane, staring at me, as if to say, "Who are you and why are you in my house?" I described what I was seeing to owner Mr. Jackson, and he showed me an old photo of Henry Saulnier, who indeed, walked with a cane and very much resembled the man I described in the front room.

Photo of Lydia Pennell.

We did not encounter Lydia on our first visit or any of our subsequent visits. In spite of this, everyone I have spoken with regarding the haunting insists that Lydia does haunt the place. Maybe Lydia is a quieter spirit, just watching over things and just unable to leave the home she once cherished so much. The only encounter I have heard involving Lydia was the oft-repeated, but never verified, claim that one man who was dining there saw the reflection of Lydia in a white Victorian dress in the men's room mirror. When the diner turned around to look at the woman, the spirit vanished.

During its restaurant days, it was easy to see why someone would want to stay forever. The house was beautifully decorated and the atmosphere was cheerful and cordial. The owners were quite comfortable with the spirit presences there, and had no wish to send them away. The price of these unseen guests was relatively cheap compared to the atmosphere and attention these spirits brought.

The house was built in 1740, and was added to in 1861. In the late 1940s, the building was used as a retirement home. In 1968, it first opened as a restaurant. Lydia Pennel inhabited the home in the mid 1800s. It was her husband that enlarged the house to the size it is today. Unfortunately, her husband died unexpectedly, and even though she did her best to hold on to her home, she was forced to sell. Her spirit is seen most often in the second floor room, now called the Lydia Room, which was once her bedroom.

The Third Floor Mystery

So what is the ghost on the third floor? Who was he? When did he live there? We may never be able to ascertain his identity. The third floor used to be the servant's quarters during the time the house was a residence. Later, it was used as living quarters for the restaurant owners. This is where the real haunting is.

On one occasion, a young man who was a relative of the owners reported that a shadowy form tried to envelop him as he slept in the third floor bedroom. At another time, the owner was resting in this same room. His pet German Shepherd had followed him there. Suddenly, the dog began barking and growling at the door to the room. The dog began backing up, then started to whine. It tore across the room and leapt through and then out the third floor window to his death! The man saw nothing during this incident, but was understandably disturbed by it.

The new owners related another incident. One of the Jackson brothers' girlfriends went to sleep in a third floor bedroom. She was awakened by footsteps crossing the room. Assuming this was her boyfriend, she was not alarmed. She heard the footsteps walk over to the bed, felt someone get into bed with her, and put their an arm around her. As she relaxed to fall back asleep, she heard the unmistakable sound of her boyfriend's vehicle pulling up outside. She jumped out of bed and turned on the light. There was no one there. She got dressed and ran downstairs. She refused to ever return to that third floor bedroom.

When we met the Finleys there, we asked about the third-floor spirit. They didn't know much about it, so we decided to just go up and have a look. As we went to the second floor landing and looked up the stairs to the third floor, Mrs. Finley let out a gasp, "Oh my gosh!" she exclaimed and pointed at the next landing, "Look at that!"

All I saw was a pile of chairs. "What's wrong?" I asked.

"Well, we were just up there before you arrived and the chairs were against the wall. We walked right by them. Now they are piled like a barricade!"

"Look like someone wants to keep us out," I said. "I think we should go see why."

We went cautiously up the stairs to the third floor. We didn't see anything, but the atmosphere was heavy and vaguely threatening. As we entered one bedroom, the door flew shut and hit my associate, Faith, in the back. This action was repeated two more times, but it did not happen when one of the men entered the room.

When we went back downstairs to discuss what we were sensing, a man came to the door claiming to have been a bartender when the Jacksons owned it. He wanted to know what was going on with the place. Of course, we asked him about the haunting. He related the typical stories about place settings being piled on tables and Lydia being seen in the bathroom mirror. We asked him about the third floor. He said he had never been allowed up there, but he had heard that it was haunted by something bad. We invited him to go up and see the area since it was empty now, but he absolutely refused and seemed very anxious to leave.

Another Eventful Visit

Our next visit to the property was marked by unexplained footsteps and voices. When we arrived, some of the group were already there but we couldn't find them. I figured they were busy exploring the grounds, so I waited out front. As they came around the corner of the house with Mrs. Finley, they asked us if we had heard anything. I said, "No, just your voices as you got closer."

They said that they had all heard a woman scream as they were looking at the back of the house. It sounded like it came from the front, so they came back to check. Of course, we at the front of the house had heard nothing.

Later, we were on the second floor in the back of the building when Faith and I distinctly heard footsteps walk across the landing and run up the stairs to the third floor. Faith and I called the rest of the group to come and check for a possible intruder, but there was no one there. This happened again when we were in the basement. We heard someone walking in another section, and upon checking, found that there was no one there.

It seemed as of the spirits were getting restless. Perhaps all of the destruction that was going on disturbed them. It is unlikely that the spirits will calmly accept the demolition of their home. Instead, they seem to be getting more active.

The new owners have kept me updated on paranormal events that they experience there. When Mrs. Finley was taking down one of the pictures in a dining room, she heard someone walk in. Assuming it was her husband, she asked him to help her. Perturbed

Chairs blocking our way to the third floor.

when she got no response, she took the picture down and turned around to an empty room. No one had walked in.

Every night someone goes up to check on the property. During one week in the spring, each evening the wicker furniture from the front porch was placed in the driveway, blocking the car from entering. It may have been a prank, but it is remarkably similar to the chairs piled in the hallway to block entrance to the third floor.

The future of the property and the building are still in dispute. The resident spirits are still there and making their presence known on audio recordings, film, and even on video. During one of our sessions there, we recorded the image of a shadowy figure emerging from one part of the basement and disappearing into another.

After these repeated visits, I am still not sure exactly how many spirits are there. I know I have not encountered the spirit of Lydia, and I am not convinced that she was ever there. What I *am* sure about is the spirits that are there are determined to stay and protect their space. Isn't that what any of us would do?

Two girls and an unseen companion look out the third floor window.

Chapter 13

Episcopal Cemetery

Concord, Pennyslvania

I have never understood why a ghost would want to haunt a graveyard. If I were a ghost, it is the last place I would want to spend the afterlife. Apparently, ghosts do not follow this line of thinking and may often be found lingering around the graveyards they were buried in. It seems that old graveyards are more likely than newer ones to have spirit activity.

I was first called to this cemetery by the son of the caretaker. He was an acquaintance of mine who had heard that I was interested in ghosts, so he invited me to come and see the graveyard next to where he lived. He told me that it was definitely haunted, claiming to see weird lights and shadows when he was outside the church and when walking the grounds at night.

According to Saint John's Episcopal Church, "This church was founded in 1702, as there were then enough inhabitants and converts in the area that an organized church was needed. The first church building was a log structure and was located where the graveyard is now. The present church building was built on the hill above the old church site in 1844."

The Battle of Brandywine occurred in 1777, less than ten miles away. Local legend holds that soldiers from both sides were buried in unmarked graves. When I visited the Newlin Grist Mill, the guide there also told me that there were soldiers from the Battle of Brandywine buried in this cemetery in unmarked graves. There is also no record of where the parishioners who died before 1844 were buried, and there are no grave markers in the cemetery that date before the early 1800s. Either they were buried somewhere else, or they are buried in unmarked graves. Perhaps this is a source of unrest in the cemetery.

Consider this: The original church building was where the cemetery is now. That church was there from 1702 until the present building was constructed in 1844. So where are the soldiers' unmarked graves? They would have to be either where the church is, where the parking lot is, or where the minister's house is now. There is also no record of the graves being moved, so when they decided to start building a big new church sixty-seven years after the battle, did they even know where these unmarked graves were? The guide at the mill said that, as far as he knows, the caretakers there "have an idea" of where they are. I know from speaking to at least one caretaker who lived there that there was no knowledge of where these graves might be. My inquiries to the church office were unanswered.

I visited this cemetery several times over a period of two years. There are always strange temperature fluctuations and shifts in light and shadow. Most of these things happen in the one end of the cemetery that is bordered by woods.

A Dowsing Visit

Due to my concern about the unmarked graves, I took dowsing rods with me. Dowsing rods are two L-shaped rods made of a lightweight metal. They are held in the hands of the dowser while he or she concentrates on what he or she is looking for. Dowsing rods can be used to locate energy or ley lines, ghosts, unmarked graves, buried or hidden objects, and water. There was one section of the cemetery where these rods kept crossing every time I passed. This indicated to me that there was possibly an unmarked grave. The part in question is in the oldest section of the cemetery in an area where there is a gap between stones

I asked the caretaker on this occasion if it was possible for there to be unmarked graves in this cemetery. He said no, but then qualified it by adding that it was a very old cemetery. Many people did not have permanent grave markers, especially in the 1600s and early 1700s, unless they were very wealthy. Most burial sites were left unmarked or were marked with fieldstones, wood posts, wood crosses, or mounds of earth, which would have long since disappeared.

That night, as I was reviewing the audio tape of my visit to the cemetery, I heard an unusual female voice on the tape. I rewound and turned it up. It was not my voice, but it was definitely a woman's voice. I was the only woman there that night. What she said reinforced my feeling of misplaced graves. The voice says clearly, "I don't know where I am."

One of the gaps in the old section.

...And Then There Was Light...

One night, I was finally able to see the weird cemetery lights that I'd heard about for myself. A friend and I were sitting in my car, facing the cemetery. I can't remember what we were talking about, but it wasn't ghosts or anything paranormal. Suddenly, I noticed a greenish light over one of the graves.

"What's that?" I asked my friend.

He looked in the direction I was pointing. "I don't know," he answered.

"You see it, though," I said.

"Yes," he replied hesitantly.

I was impatient. "Well, go over and see what it is." He looked at me with wide, frightened eyes.

"No way am I going over there," he said quietly.

Area where the EVP was recorded.

We both sat and looked at the light for the next forty-five minutes or so. When I thought about getting out of the car, I was so overcome with a feeling of dread that I doubt I could have gotten out of the car, even if it was on fire. The light never moved or changed in size or color during the entire time we observed it. When it became clear that the light wasn't going anywhere, my friend asked me to go around to the side of the building so he could run into his apartment, which was located in the basement level of the church. He and his family were the caretakers of the property."

I know some people will say that it was swamp gas from rotting vegetation. The trouble with that theory is that my friend checked the next day to find that no rotting vegetation of any kind could be found on the grave where we observed the light—or any of the graves nearby. In addition, the theory of swamp gas itself is still rather controversial. According to an article in *Pursuit Magazine*, in order for the gas to glow, it would have to be ignited. There was no source of ignition. There was also no characteristic pop of releasing gas.

That was the only time I visually saw anything in this cemetery, but I have been able to capture unexplained lights and mist with my camera.

SLAM!

On another occasion we were sitting at the edge of the parking lot overlooking the cemetery. The church building was behind us. Suddenly, we heard a door slam shut. When we looked behind us, there was nothing. We shrugged it off and began talking again.

SLAM! There it was again. We wondered what door was shutting because there was no one else around and all the lights in the church behind and the minister's house to our left were out.

SLAM! Again, the door slammed. This time we were both positive it was coming from the church. As one of the caretakers, my friend felt obligated to go and check the church to make sure everything was all right. He asked me to come with him to stand outside the door that we felt was the source of the noise while he went around to the back door, which was the only door he had a key to.

I admit, I was a bit nervous standing there in the dark, alone, but at the same time I was hoping that something would happen. The door began to open slowly. It was my friend.

"Well," he said, "no one's here. I looked through all the rooms and found nothing. Everyone's asleep and has been. My brother is awake downstairs working on something and my parents would have had to walk by him to get upstairs."

We weren't sure what to think, so we just decided to go sit back down and see what happened. This time, though, we were watching the church doors. Of course, nothing happened. After a while I got up to leave and he walked me to my car. His back

Ectoplasmic mist above the tombstones.

was to the church and I reached up to give him a goodbye hug. Over his shoulder I saw the church door open and then slam shut—the same noise we had heard earlier! I tried to keep my voice down as I said, "I saw it! It was the church door! Your brother must be playing around with us."

He looked toward the door and said, "I don't want to scare you, but he can't be doing it. When I came back up to check the church, I locked the doors from inside the church as I went out. He can't open them. I have the keys." He held them up, jingling them in the air to show me.

As if someone was listening, SLAM! There went the same door. This time we both saw it slamming shut.

I have to say, aside from the door being locked anyway, that there is no way the door could have been blowing open and closed. This was one of those heavy doors with the push bar and catch. When the church was not having services, the door was always set to lock so that it couldn't be opened from the outside. Also, I was with my friend when he shut the door to come back out. The door was securely closed. Fortunately, I wasn't the one who had to now go back in there and check things again!

Stranger Than the Grave?

Back to my initial question; why would a ghost want to haunt a graveyard? Until we understand what ghosts are, we will never understand why we encounter them in the places we do. One theory about graveyards says that older graveyards are often haunted because the sites for them were chosen because of an eerie or uncomfortable atmosphere. In other words, it seemed like a good place to put a graveyard. This theory is supported by the large number of anomalous photos containing orbs, vortices, and paranormal fogs or mists. Perhaps the eerie feeling in these areas is due to the presence of an entry way or portal to the next world. Since it is, in theory, easiest for ghosts to cross between the worlds there, it is logical that this is a place where they would be found.

Another reason for the abundance of ghost sightings in graveyards is that is where we, for some reason, think they should be. If we look for something mostly in one type of place, we are likely to find more of them in that place. For example, say you walk along the sidewalk with your head down because you find money there. This doesn't mean that money is naturally attracted to the pavement; it just means that you find it there most often because you look for it there most often. Further, the ghosts in graveyards tend to be the type that I refer to as intelligent hauntings. As such, maybe they appear there because they know that in a graveyard they are more likely to come across a living person that is looking for a ghost.

Also, the graveyard is where we go to visit our loved ones. Most of us go there and talk to the family members and friends at their final resting place. A great deal of energy is focused on the deceased people at that location. All this energy focused on them might actually draw them there, especially if it is an easy crossover point for them.

Another reason we may encounter more ghosts at graveyards, especially old ones, is because disturbance of a burial site seems to draw the person's spirit back. My theory for this is that the act of burial and the ceremonies involved must form some type of seal or closure for the spirit. When that seal is broken or disturbed, it may reopen some type of connection between the spirit world and our world.

If that is the case here, I hope that the replacement of grave markers and general cleanup of the cemetery has helped some of the spirits find peace.

Chapter 14

The Old Riviera Farmhouse

Concord Township, Pennsylvania

A haunting in the office can really make the workday interesting! This particular office was originally a farmhouse on Concord Road in Concord Township, Pennsylvania. Like Thornbury Township, Concord was also once part of Chester County and was part of the original land grant given to William Penn. It was called Concord because "of the harmonious feelings which prevailed among settlers here." When this house was built, it was surrounded by fields and pastures. Now, it is surrounded by modern housing developments and a busy roadway.

As usual, when I pulled up to the house with two companions, I knew nothing about the history or the details of the haunting, but the age of the building was apparent. As we walked toward the front door, my attention was drawn to a window high up on the side of the house. The feeling of someone staring down at me from that window was so strong that when the manager greeted us to let us in, I asked him who was in the building. He replied that there was no one there and that he had come alone. I couldn't resist another glance at that window before we entered, but I couldn't see anyone. The house wasn't giving up its secrets yet.

As we walked into the house, I noted that it looked like a typical office, with smaller offices on one side and a large conference room on the other side of a central hallway that was dominated by a central staircase. Behind the stairs was a modern kitchen and under the stairs was a door that drew my attention.

A Shock in the Basement

"Where does this go?" I asked the manager, pointing at the door.

"To more offices in the basement," he replied.

I had to go down there. We opened the door and I peered into the darkness below me. I was followed slowly down the stairs by another investigator and our videographer. When I reached the bottom of the stairs, I turned to my right.

I am ashamed to admit this, but at this point, I screamed at the top of my voice. There was a tall man with dark hair and extremely pale skin standing right in front of me. In retrospect, I cannot say what caused me to react this way, but as soon as my gaze met his, I was overcome by a feeling of absolute terror and panic. I turned and ran back up the stairs, nearly falling over the investigator who was behind me, and nearly knocked over the videographer in my rush to get as far away from the scene as possible.

When I reached the kitchen I stopped to catch my breath and check on my associates. Of course, they all wanted to

The exterior of the Riviera Farmhouse.

know what the heck happened. As I described what I had seen, I could tell from the looks on their faces that they hadn't seen anything. There was nothing on the video, either. Nevertheless, I knew what I had seen and hoped for some confirmation from someone. Thankfully, the manager spoke up.

"What did the man look like?" he asked.

"Well," I said, "he was about this tall (I held up my hand to indicate a height), and had dark, short, curly hair, and very pale skin."

The manager then proceeded to tell us that the description sounded very much like his former boss, who had been very dedicated to the business and often worked long hours in the basement office. It seemed logical to him that his former boss would want to check on things, especially if there were strangers in the building. The man had died very unexpectedly and rather quickly from cancer. "But," he then offered, "there has been weird stuff happening ever since we started using this as an office. Employees would report strange things to me on a regular basis."

Apparently the house had more secrets to reveal.

File cabinet blocking door.

We returned to the basement. This time our entry was completely uneventful. As we walked through the basement, though, I noticed something odd. On one of the walls, there was an old door with a big file cabinet in front of it.

"Why is that cabinet there?" I asked the manager.

He replied with a smile, "I was wondering if you would notice that. We keep the cabinet in front of there because the door keeps opening by itself. It was a little disturbing to the people that work down here."

Of course, I had to see what was behind that door. Hoping for no more nasty surprises, we moved the cabinet and opened it. It was a little disappointing. There was no dark tunnel, secret room, or swirling, misty form emerging from the darkness. There was simply a flight of stairs leading to an old, damp storage-type area with a dirt floor. We stood in there for a while, but nothing happened, so we decided to continue exploring the building. I was thinking that the door opening was more of a structural problem than a ghostly one.

Don't Go in the Attic!

I was anxious to get upstairs and see the window where I'd had the feeling of being watched. As soon as we entered the attic room that held the mysterious window, we all felt a change in the temperature and the atmosphere. The temperature in the attic was noticeably lower and registered from 8 – 12 degrees Fahrenheit colder than the ambient temperature of the rest of the house. I tried to take a photo and my camera shut itself off. When I turned it back on, I saw that the batteries were dead. Telling the group that my batteries had just died, I walked back to the center of the room. (It looked like I would have to wait to get my photo of the window.)

Right at that moment, I felt the air next to me grow even colder and I started to feel that tingly, prickly sensation on my back and neck that I associate with a spirit presence. I began to describe what I was feeling as well as the images that were coming to mind regarding what type of spirit was there, when I felt the coldness pass right next to me and then continue behind me. I turned my head towards the source as it dissipated behind me. Although I hadn't seen anything, the video camera picked up what I was sensing. As I was talking and following the cold spot, the video clearly showed a white, undulating, misty shape passing by my side. (You can view this video at: http://www.willyoubelieve.com/concord_large.avi.)

We returned to the conference room to share what we had just experienced and to change the batteries in our equipment. The other investigators and I agreed that we had all felt *something* in the attic. I felt as though the spirit in the attic was female and that she had been employed there as some type of domestic help. The impression I had of her was that she could cause electrical disturbances in the attic and that she would mainly make herself known by turning lights on and off. When I tried to connect with her, I had a feeling of not being able to breathe, almost a suffocating feeling, as if she suffered from asthma or some kind of disease that made it difficult to breathe. One of the other investigators stated that she had an impression of mischievous children running around the second floor of the house.

As we began to share our thoughts, the manager brought over an antique photo of the farmhouse. The caption on the photo read, "This picture was taken about 1895. The woman on the left is Lavinia S. Field with her daughter Mary M. Field (approx. 12 years old). Mary later married Frank P. Valentine.

He then continued to relate what he and others had experienced in the old farmhouse. He started out by saying that we were dead on; the attic seemed to be the most active place in the house for paranormal activity. He and others often heard footsteps and doors slamming there. In addition, there were constant unexplained electrical problems in the attic. Lights would turn on and off by themselves. Electrical equipment would stop working for no reason. He said it took all of his strength not to tell us this when I announced that my batteries died while we were in that area.

Take a Seat...Ring a Bell

In addition to the electrical disturbances and unexplained sounds, they also experienced furniture moving around on its own in the first floor conference room. One day, he had set up the chairs around the conference table for a meeting. He went to get something from an office, and when he returned, all of the chairs had been moved away from the table pushed against one wall. He quickly rearranged the chairs and tried to forget about it. The spirits then made sure he would remember.

On another day, he was up in the attic changing a filter on the HVAC system. He was alone in the building at the time, so he was shocked to find that as he returned downstairs, once again, all of the chairs that had been arranged around the conference table were pushed against the wall. Obviously someone has their own ideas about how the furniture should be arranged!

He then related an incident that was significant because there were two independent witnesses—police officers! That night he had closed up as usual; locking the doors and setting the alarm. As he was putting his things in his vehicle, a police car pulled up. Two officers stepped out and told him that they were responding to the alarm that had gone off. A bit perplexed, but chalking this up to another "electrical disturbance" he went back and unlocked the door so the police could make sure the building was secure.

They walked through the whole building, even the attic, but there was no one there. He reset the alarm and locked the door while the officers were checking the perimeter. As they were all returning to their vehicles, they heard a huge crash from inside the building, as if a 200 – 300-pound object had been dropped onto the floor. The officers ran back to the building to check it out, but, as before, they found nothing out of the ordinary.

The officers finally left, shaking their heads in disbelief. For the manager, it was good to finally have someone who didn't work there, and hadn't heard about any of the unexplained happenings, to have experienced something like that.

Then Who?

Who haunts the old farmhouse office? A servant? Mischievous children? A dedicated former supervisor? Perhaps there is something about this place in Concord, something so harmonious that people continue to stay after death.

Before we left, the manager shared one more thing that had happened at the house. One spring day there was a fatal accident right in front of the building. The driver, a teenage girl, had been ejected from her vehicle and she landed on the lawn. The vehicle itself smashed through the white picket fence that bordered the yard and landed on top of her, pinning her beneath it. According to the manager, she was killed instantly and then her body laid there for over an hour on their lawn before anyone could get the car out of there. This tragedy happened shortly after his former boss passed away.

I asked him if there had been an increase in the intensity of events after these incidents, and he said that he had never experienced anything in the house until after these things happened.

Author Snippet!

It is known that the roads in Concord are among the most dangerous in the state. They are full of dips, sudden turns, and blind spots. In fact, Concord Township contains the second busiest intersection in the state, the intersection of Routes 1 and 202, called "Painter's Crossing" after the Brandywine Valley School of painters, notably Andrew and N. C. Wyeth.

Concord is also the home of the second deadliest one-car accident in the history of the state. Early on Mother's Day in 1994, a car containing five students from nearby Sun Valley School District went airborne after speeding over one of the many dips along Smithbridge Road. The car hit a tree and the five teens were killed. This accident has also been the source of a haunting on Smithbridge Road. Although I have never seen anything paranormal, during my research for this book, I was told by several local people that the spot where this accident happened is haunted by the spirit of one of the victims.

Chapter 15

Haunted Barn

Thornton, Pennsylvania

In the field of paranormal research, you get calls and e-mails from all types of people. One group of people that we get a fair number of calls from is building contractors. One call, in particular, resulted in one of the most memorable and compelling experiences I have ever had as an investigator.

I received an e-mail from a building inspector who wanted to speak with me because he had some questions about a property he was working with. He believed that the property he was currently inspecting was haunted and he wanted to know whether the things he experienced were his imagination or not. (We get a lot of e-mails and calls from people who believe their homes or places of business are haunted, and most of them just want reassurance that they are not crazy or imagining things.) When I called him that night, the urgency in his voice was apparent and it quickly became clear that he needed more than reassurance.

"I know this place is haunted. I have never felt anything like this before," he said excitedly into the phone. "You have to come. I have contacted other groups and no one will come out. The place is probably going to be condemned, so you have to come out tonight." He was nearly breathless as he told me about seeing shadowy forms and hearing footsteps and other unexplained noises.

This situation should have raised a red flag for me. I am agreeing to go out to meet some strange man who claims he has a haunted barn. It has to be tonight. This place is uninhabited and out in the middle of nowhere. I finish work at 11 pm, so I will be arriving there around midnight. Perfect. Against my better judgment, I agree to meet this man on a dark road in front of an abandoned and likely haunted property in the middle of nowhere at midnight. This is beginning to sound like the beginning of a bad horror movie, yet there is something compelling that makes me want to go. (You will be happy to know that at the last minute, I finally listened to my own common sense and make a few calls, convincing a male friend of mine to accompany me. And by the way, I would never recommend or suggest that anyone else ever do anything like this. Luck was on my side that night and all ends well. It very easily could have ended badly under different circumstances.)

The exact location of this site must be withheld because it is on private property. I will say that it is a road that comes off Route 1 and it is located in Thornton, Pennsylvania. I was happy to see when we drove up to the site that I knew this road well.

We arrived at 12:15 am and were greeted by a very professional-looking man and his companion who shook our hands and made us feel instantly at ease. He led us up a dirt path towards a huge barn that loomed on the hill above us. It was very dark, because there was no electricity at all in the barn and no streetlights in this undeveloped section of the neighborhood. At this point, I knew nothing about what he had experienced there. If you recall, I prefer to go in with no information about the building or experiences. I do this to avoid having the power of suggestion color my impressions and experiences.

Entrance to the barn was through a door on the ground floor. This door led to an area containing stalls for livestock, complete with dirt, hay, bats, and a few rats. Further investigation revealed that this lower level also had a room with bunks and a refrigerated storage room. So far, we noticed nothing unusual in our preliminary assessment on the ground floor.

It was then that, our contact told us that most of the activity had occurred upstairs in the main barn area. He pointed to a narrow flight of stairs. The stairs were in very bad condition, with some missing. I chose to stay downstairs with his companion to give things a chance to develop on that level. We were not getting any significant results with our temperature and EMF reading equipment, but the feeling of being watched was absolutely overwhelming. One of the photos taken during this time by his companion revealed a misty area near the door that we had entered.

The pentagram is visible in this photo. It is painted in orange.

A Sign

We decided to go up the rickety stairs and share what we had found so far. As soon as we entered the upper level of the barn, I noticed a large pentagram painted on the floor near a door and two windows on the other side of the barn.

I began to walk around and take some general photos for reference. As if the pentagram weren't enough, right across from the pentagram, there was a jawbone nailed to one of the columns. I ran out of film and started to change the roll. As I was changing the film, something caused me to glance up. When I looked towards the upper door of the barn, I saw the shadowy form of a man standing in the doorway to the outside. He seemed to be leaning against the doorway as if he were just watching us go about our business. I hurriedly finished loading the film, and took some pictures. One of these pictures showed a light.

Now, there was no electricity at all in this barn to provide a source of light, and there were no light fixtures in place. Also, the window you see in the photograph was boarded up. It had no glass in its panes to cause a reflection from the flash. The second photo contains an orb anomaly. After the photo anomalies were captured, things began to happen more quickly.

I wanted to investigate the area where I had seen the figure. As I moved toward the area, I was overcome by a horrible lightheaded, sick, and dizzy feeling that caused me to lose my balance and I had to sit down on the floor and lean against one of the wooden beams.

My friend came over to see if I was all right, and his EMF detector jumped from a green or "safe" reading to a red "danger" reading. When I got my EMF detector out, mine began sounding a danger level alarm. These readings are not normal for paranormal activity and usually indicate either a very strong source of electromagnetic energy, such as a generator or transformer, or an equipment malfunction. We asked the contractor if there was any electricity or outlets in the beam or

Chapter 15

Unexplained light.

even in the area. He advised that there wasn't. A regular electrical outlet will not cause the meter to jump to the top. The only explanation that I can come up with is that, for some reason, both of our EMF meters, which were different styles, malfunctioned at the same time.

I was still so dizzy at that point that my friend had to help me get up and over to the stairs. As we descended, I was overcome by a feeling of panic, as if someone was right behind me and waiting to push me down the stairs or attack me physically. It was not a comfortable kind of feeling that one may experience in a haunted place. This was a negative feeling. Something up there definitely did not want to be bothered or measured and it wanted us out of there.

We continued to investigate the upstairs area. I made a point of avoiding the section where I felt dizzy. We each took a section and began walking it slowly, taking readings and trying to get a feel for what was there. We all froze as we heard footsteps downstairs followed by a loud clanging noise, as if someone were banging on a pipe with a metal object. We ran down the stairs, anxious to find the source of the sounds. As we got the bottom floor, the noise immediately stopped. One of the men stayed by the door so that no one could go out or come in while the rest of us went to investigate. At this point, we were half expecting to find a person wandering around inside with us, but we found nothing—no people or animals. What's more, we couldn't locate anything that could have been the source of the sound we heard.

We gathered in the stable area downstairs and discussed the possibilities. The only living things known to be there—besides us—were rats and bats! The clanging had been a regular, measured rhythm, and the footsteps were definitely two feet in shoes. As we continued to discuss the phenomena, the conversation shifted to a similar experience we had in Gettysburg.

We were at Little Round Top in Gettysburg and heard disembodied footsteps go past us. We started recording and asking questions. Our recorder was on voice activation, so were we were thrilled when we saw that we had a response to our questions. "Which side did you fight for?" When we played it back, a loud male voice was on the tape. "South!" the voice stated emphatically.

At that exact moment, with the word "South" dying on my lips, we all fell silent as we heard a loud thud upstairs. This was followed by heavy footsteps and a loud dragging sound. The sound went, "Drag, step, step, drag, step, step, etc." The contractor took off upstairs to investigate, and I called out to whatever was up there, "If you want to talk, talk, but please don't re-enact someone's death!" The noise stopped like someone flipped a switch as soon as the contractor reached the top floor.

We decided to call it a night at 2:30 am. As we walked away from the barn, we looked back because the feeling that someone was watching from that doorway upstairs was very, very strong. I wanted to take a photo of the outside, but my camera would not turn on. I asked my friend to take a photo, but his camera would not work either, so we didn't get a photo of the outside.

What was in the old barn? We never found out. Another paranormal group went through the barn one night and the lead investigator ended up with hives all over her body. Their conclusion was that someone had been practicing black magic there. There was a large pentagram on the floor and animal bones nailed to the wall. At least, we *hope* they were animal bones!

Enough is Enough

The contractor stayed in touch with me over the next week. His inspection found that there were termites and termite damage, but the foundation was still good. He continued to see shadows as he was taking measurements and one time when he was alone on top of a thirty-six-foot extension ladder counting beams, the ladder started to move. He took a deep breath, and continued counting the beams. Then he noticed that one of the beams was vibrating. He felt that our visit had probably stirred things up even more. As the week went by, he began to see orbs of light move through the basement area. Although this seems like enough to scare off anyone, this man stayed to try and finish his job. His resolve reached its limit one night towards the end of the week.

Since there was no electricity, he had to bring a portable generator in the bed of his truck to use his power tools. One night, he was going to use a saw up on the top floor. He had the truck parked outside, with the cord to the saw hanging from the top floor to the generator below. He started the generator and returned inside to plug in the saw. As he reached for the saw cord, the saw took of by itself across the floor.

That was it. He ran out of the barn, jumped in his truck, and drove away, dragging the generator cord behind him and leaving the saw to whatever was in the barn.

I wanted to return to the site again for a longer investigation, but the barn was then declared unsafe and taken over by the township. Now partially demolished and converted into a private home, the structure is occupied at present. Many times I have passed by the old barn and wondered if the man in the doorway is still there.

Who was he? Who or what caused the phenomena that we and the contractor witnessed? There is no history on the barn, since it wasn't an inhabited dwelling. Were the phenomena we experienced related to the pentagram we saw painted on the floor? It's possible. Most "ordinary" ghosts don't generate enough energy to make a saw take off across a floor.

And what significance did the pentagram have? Was it part of a black magic ritual or just graffiti? Without doubt, the pentagram is a powerful symbol, just like the cross or the Star of David. The pentagram, just like any other powerful symbol, can be used to generate constructive or destructive energy. In this case, the presence of bones in the vicinity of the pentagram is a strong indicator that some type of black magic was performed there. In addition, pagans and Wiccans who practice white magic don't go to barns and paint pentagrams on the floor. They prefer to perform their rites outdoors when possible, and would never, ever vandalize someone else's property.

Does It Really Happen?

Okay, so do people really go into abandoned buildings, paint pentagrams on floors, and perform black magic or Satanic rituals? The answer is, "Yes, they do." For example, in July of 1991, the Commonwealth of Pennsylvania prosecuted a group of people for false imprisonment during their participation in what was described as a Satanic ritual. The victim stated he was an unwilling participant and was taken against his will to an *abandoned barn* and tied to stakes in the ground over a pentagram.

A satanic ritual was performed over him. A leather collar with nails embedded was placed around his neck. During the ritual, one of the participants pressed on the nails in the collar to puncture his skin, put his fingers in the victim's blood, and then touched it to his lips.

The victim was fortunately released after being warned he'd be killed if he told anyone. Some of the evidence in the case against those involved included skulls and books that were found in their homes.

In light of this, "It cannot be denied that, here and there, there have been and continue to be, in the countryside (in the open, in caves, in desecrated chapels) or in urban peripheral areas (ruined buildings, abandoned structures and premises) traces that prove the celebration, strictly nocturnal, of Satanic ceremonies." These rituals can open portals or vortices that allow all kinds of low-level spirits into our world. In the course of your investigations, please be very cautious when you see any evidence of Satanic or black-magic rituals. The spirits associated with these rituals are not human and can be very dangerous.

Chapter 16

The Heilbron Mansion

Rose Tree, Pennsylvania

My first visit to this mansion was in 1986, when I was sixteen years old. After that visit, I was hooked. I had read the book, *Night Stalks the Mansion*, by Harold Cameron and Constance Westbie, and was fascinated by the prospect of a genuine haunted house not far from where I lived. That fall, one of my male friends mentioned that he knew where the mansion was. He said that kids went up there all the time and offered to take me that weekend.

When we drove up to the house, I was skeptical. It was obviously abandoned and empty, but it didn't look haunted. At one time, this had been a gorgeous home. Even if there were no ghosts, it would be great to see the inside of this formerly grand estate. We parked around the back of the house and started to walk towards the front door. As we approached the house, I looked up at the big windows on the second and third floors. "Which one of these windows did the former mistress hang herself from?" I wondered.

For those who have not read the book about this house, I highly recommend that you do. It is a well-written and intriguing account of one family's experience with the ghosts with whom they shared their home. According to the book, the family that lived in the house in the mid-nineteenth century had a beautiful young daughter who went away to some type of finishing school. When she returned one summer, she was lured from the house, raped, and murdered by one of the stable hands. Her body was found in Ridley Creek, just down the hill from the house. The stable hand was lynched and hanged by the other servants from a tree on the property. The mother of the girl had a nervous breakdown and hung herself from one of the large front windows of the house. All the makings of a good ghost story, with several candidates for a haunting!

As we walked into the front door, I related a similar version of the history to my companions. "Cool!" they said, "Let's see which window it was!" They ran off up the front stairs, leaving me staring at the hallway to my right which led to a library. I stood, thinking back to the book. The library was supposed to be one of the really haunted spots. As I tried to work up the nerve to enter the dark room alone, I heard footsteps approaching me from the direction of the library. Frozen with disbelief, I peered into the shadows. Although I couldn't see anyone, there

Front view of the mansion.

was no mistaking the sound of footsteps approaching. I tried to call out to my friends, but couldn't. The footsteps seemed to pass right by me and up the stairs. They continued on up those stairs towards where I knew my friends were. Finally, finding the power to move, I started up the steps in front of me, calling out, "Hey! I heard something!"

At that moment, the most bizarre thing happened. I heard a loud *Whoosh!* sound followed by a tremendous crash. It sounded like someone had dropped about a thousand aluminum soda cans from the ceiling onto one of the upper floors. I heard my friends yelling, "What was that? Did you hear that?" They ran towards the landing and down the stairs. This time I didn't linger. We all ran out the door, back to the car, and sped out of there. As we drove home, we all wondered what it could have been. We started to feel kind of silly for being scared by a noise, but I knew it wasn't just a noise. I told them about the footsteps I heard right before that.

The guys wanted to go back and see what caused the noise. After a few minutes of half-hearted protestations, I agreed to return, as long as I didn't have to go in. I sat in the car and watched them walk back to the house. I saw the lights from their flashlights shining

If there really was a suicide from a window, it was this one.

through the empty windows as they searched for the source of the crash. They returned a few minutes later with puzzled looks on their faces.

"Weird! We looked all over the house and all we found was one Coke can rolling around on the third floor! There was nothing there that could have made that noise."

Yes, it was weird. I returned to the house several times over the next few months. When warmer weather arrived, I didn't go up there as much because there were always people there partying at night. Even though my first visit there had been a little "weird," at my subsequent visits, I found the house to be a pretty peaceful place. The only areas where I felt any kind of negative feelings were in the basement and next to the third floor window.

Is the Heilbron Mansion Haunted?

This question *should* be in the past tense, because the mansion that I visited as a teenager burned down one night in June of 1987. The property was purchased by a developer and a semblance of the former mansion was rebuilt on the foundation and stands there today.

I have not returned to the mansion since it burned down, but I receive e-mails about the mansion on a regular basis from other people who, like me, visited the mansion when they were teenagers. All of them swear the house was haunted. But haunted by whom?

Harold Cameron stated in his book that the mansion was haunted by the stable hand, whose footsteps could be heard crunching on the gravel path between the coach house and the front steps, and the mother, whose presence was felt in the library. In the book, he made a deal with the ghost that if they would stay out of the library, she would leave them alone. One night, a guest of theirs went into the library and fell asleep. The entire house was awakened by what sounded like the heater exploding. Upon investigation, all they found was a book on the floor of the library, which had fallen from the hands of the dozing guest. Their theory was that the ghost was somehow able to amplify the sound of the book to show them her displeasure with the trespasser. Is it possible that this is what happened to us that night in

Back of the Mansion.

Side view of the Mansion.

1986? Did the ghost amplify the sound of one can to warn us away from the house?

If so, then there is at least one ghost that haunted the old mansion. Was it the mother of the unfortunate girl? We may never know. The historical records of the property contain no record of a murder of any member of the Edwards family, who occupied the mansion from 1776 until 1828. In fact, the eldest Edwards daughter, Elizabeth, who would have been the correct age for the incident described in the book, and even has the correct name (in the book she is called Lisa), lived to adulthood and died in Philadelphia when she was twenty-four years old. Records indicate that her mother did commit suicide in 1802, when Elizabeth would have been sixteen years old. Is this the source of the haunting? Does the depressed spirit of a mother still linger at the site of her suicide, consumed by guilt?

Chapter 17

A Victorian House in Media

I was asked to come to a home to do psychic readings for a bachelorette party. The house was a Victorian twin on the south end of downtown Media. When I entered the house, I was greeted by the hostess and was immediately struck by the feeling that there was spirit activity here. I asked her about the history of the house and she said they had just bought it a year ago, so she didn't know too much about it. I asked if I could look around for a little bit until they were ready to get started. Understandably proud of her new home, the hostess offered to give me the grand tour and off we went!

The first floor had a formal living room with a large fireplace and carved mantle. There was also a large dining room, very nicely decorated in a Victorian style, as well as a modernized kitchen. In the kitchen, I began to get that tingly feeling on the back of my neck. When I turned around, I saw a narrow doorway in the wall behind me.

"What's this?" I asked, pulling the door open. "Oh," she replied, "That's just the back stairs." There was a tall first step up to the stairs, which were the typical narrow, steep, twisting back stairs used by servants. Intrigued, I stepped onto the stairs and began to climb.

I have often wondered about the design of servants' stairs. Why are they so dark, narrow, steep, and twisting? Is this a space-saving measure? I have gone up and down countless numbers of them in old houses I am called to investigate, and I can't help but think that if I were using these stairs, it would only be a matter of time before I would lose my footing on them and end up in a crumpled heap at the bottom of them. How many servants have ended up the same way? Surprisingly, I have never encountered a ghost that was the result of such a fall!

As I carefully went up the stairs, I was sure that I was on the trail of a spirit. The trail led me to the third floor landing. At the top of the stairs, there was a door that entered the landing. Immediately opposite was the front staircase, and there were two doors on our right, and one down the hall facing us.

"Well," she said, "That's where I want you to do the readings. It's kind of like my sitting room, where I go to think or read."

We proceeded along the hallway towards the room. As we passed the first doorway, I felt a cool breeze go by. I asked her if there were drafts in the house.

She replied, "Well, it is an old house. If you get too cold in the room you are in, I will move you downstairs."

I began to wonder at this point why she was putting me on the third floor to begin with. The downstairs living and dining rooms were quite large and the kitchen had a table that would have been suitable for my purposes. So I asked her, "Wouldn't you rather have me downstairs so the girls don't have to go up and down the stairs to get their readings?"

"No", she answered, "I thought you would have more privacy up here. It's quieter, too, so you can focus more on the readings!" That seemed reasonable to me, so I went on to the next question.

"What do you use the rooms up here for?" I asked.

"The first one is my husband's office," she said, pointing at the door next to the servant's stairs, "and the other is for storage right now."

"So no one lives or sleeps up here?"

"No, not right now."

"Does that mean someone used to sleep up here?"

"Well, we used to have a roommate when we first bought the house. His room was where the office is now. He only stayed here a few months and then he moved out."

"Why?" she asked, worriedly, "Are you picking something up about him? Is he okay?"

"Nothing like that," I assured her. "I was just trying to sort things out up here. There are a lot of different energies."

When I said that, she laughed. "Oh, I'll bet," she said, still chuckling, "This house was shared by a bunch of actors. You should have seen the place! What a mess! I don't even want to think about what went on here."

At that, I told her I could just stay up there and get settled in the room. She could send the first person up in about ten minutes.

Strange Readings

I began setting up my reading area, which includes a blue cloth, a small quartz crystal sphere, a blue candle and a white candle, a goddess icon, and my tarot cards. I lit some sandalwood incense and the candles, closed my eyes, and settled back into the soft chair to get centered and prepared to read.

"Creeeeeeeeaaaaaaaak!" My eyes flew open and I looked toward the door.

"Hello?" I called, thinking someone had come up.

When there was no answer, I got up and looked into the hallway. It was empty. I stood there for a few seconds, closed my eyes, and tried to see if there was anything else there—something not apparent to the conscious mind. Voices erupted with laughter and ice clinked in glasses on the landing below. "The party is really getting started, I thought, "I better get myself ready."

I went back into the room and noticed that the room was ice cold. Both candles had gone out. *There must be some draft here,* I thought to myself as I heard footsteps on the front stairs. I quickly relit the candles.

"Hi!" said a cute girl in her early twenties. "You are the psychic?" she asked.

"Yes," I replied.

"Wow!" she said, "I thought you'd be older!"

We both had a laugh at that, and I settled down to the reading. It was hard to concentrate. I kept hearing the creaking noise on the landing. Since no one else said anything, I assumed it was something I was picking up on that no one else was hearing.

After a couple hours, I was getting tired and the hostess came up with the bride for her reading. They were both very happy and excited about the readings. They wanted to hear each other's, so we settled down in the chairs and got started.

Sure enough, the creaking began. This time, though, I noticed that the hostess looked toward the door.

"Do you hear that?" I asked her.

"I think so. It's like a creaking noise, right?"

"Yes," I said, "I have been hearing it all evening. What is it?"

"I don't know," she said.

The bride jumped up. "Let's go see what it is. It's probably something stupid."

The hostess hesitated, but I followed the bride-to-be into the hallway.

We both noticed that the office door was slightly ajar.

"Was it like that when you came up?" I asked her.

"I don't think so," she said. We called to the hostess, who was still sitting in the room.

"Was this door open?"

"What door?"

"The office."

She came running out of the room. "No", she answered. The she said quietly, "He always keeps it closed..." Her voice trailed off at this point.

We both looked at her, expectantly.

"Okay," she finally admitted, "he even locks the door, but it always comes open. We don't know why. He says it is some funny thing with the door not sitting right."

"Can we go in?" I asked her.

"Sure," she said. She didn't follow us.

In the room there were computers and printers, file cabinets, stacks of papers, boxes full of files, and other things that would be in any home office.

There was also a presence—I was feeling that cold and clammy sensation I often get when there is a spirit in the room.

"Do you feel anything?" I asked the bride.

"It feels weird," she said, "Kind of cold and…well, weird!" I decided to go back into the hallway to talk to the hostess.

I told her what happened since I had been there. She just nodded the whole time. Then she admitted that she had put me up there to see what would happen.

When they'd bought the house, they'd had her husband's brother move in to help them out. He got the third floor all to himself, but he moved out after three months, saying he couldn't sleep. He said he kept having weird dreams about an older African-American woman in a white cap bending over him as he slept.

After he moved out, he admitted that it wasn't really a dream. *He had actually seen her several times when he knew he was awake!*

I asked the hostess if she had ever seen her. She said that she hadn't seen her up there, but had seen something many times out of the corner of her eye as she worked in the kitchen.

We went back in the hallway and we heard the creak again as the bride-to-be stepped on the section of floor in front of the back stairs. That was the creak that we had been hearing all night.

I never found out the identity of this spirit and what the reason for her continued presence there. The homeowner seemed relieved by my assurance that there was a spirit though, and that it wasn't hostile. They chose to leave things as they were, as many people do in cases like this.

A Word About Servants

In smaller households, it was likely that there was just one servant—a "maid-of-all-work" She was typically a very young girl, whose day began at 6:00 or 6:30 am and ended about 11:00 pm. She was responsible for all of the duties, which would be completed by a huge staff of servants in larger households. These duties included housemaid, nursemaid, parlor maid, chambermaid, cook, lady's maid, and the like. Thus, she was expected to do all of the scrubbing, cleaning, cooking, caring for children sweeping, dusting, and on and on, that was required by each of those positions.

Servants were essential for households with social pretensions and defined the social status of those they worked for. They played a substantial role not only in the homes of their masters, but in the lives of the children and other servants, if they were any.

In the United States, servants in the middle-class household of the Victorian Era were often Irish immigrants and African Americans. Many former slaves, who had escaped to the North, and places like Pennsylvania, then found work as paid servants. Harriet Tubman was one famous example of this.

Since these servants or maids of all work were such a huge and integral part of the lives of the families they served, it is not difficult to see that a truly dedicated and loving maid would find herself unable to abandon her duties to her household as long as the house was inhabited. I believe that this is why there are so many hauntings involving ghosts of servants in homes that once employed them.

Chapter 18

A Spirit at the Office

Media, Pennsylvania

Once people find out that I am an active paranormal investigator, they feel comfortable sharing their stories with me. One night, I was at a holiday party and started chatting with a woman who was a realtor. She had an office in an old house in Media. Our conversation began typically; she asked, "How can you tell if a place is haunted?"

"Well," I replied, "usually people will hear footsteps when no one else is there, or lights will turn off or on, doors open and close, objects get moved, things like that."

"I think our office might be haunted," she confided. She then related a typical series of events that included misplaced papers, files, phones not working for no reason, lights going on and off, and doors opening and closing by themselves. She asked me what they could do about it.

I had to tell her that what she was experiencing was very typical, and nothing to be alarmed about. I understood that it was annoying and sometimes frightening to have these things happen, but it sounded to me like someone was just making themselves at home and trying to get attention. I gave her my card and told her that if she wanted me to stop over and check it out for her, I would be happy to. She took the card and we went back to mingling.

I didn't hear from her for a few months. I wasn't surprised that she didn't call because most of the time when people ask me about phenomena that they are experiencing, what they really want is acknowledgement that it was not their imaginations, and reassurance that what happened was not meant to harm them.

So I was surprised to receive a call from her. She sounded very excited. "I just had to tell you what happened with our ghost!" she said.

"All right," I replied, "I can't wait to hear it."

"We hired a new receptionist after Christmas and right away she started asking if the place was haunted. I wasn't sure what to say to her at first, but after a while, she was so insistent, we just decided to tell her some of the things we had experienced at the office. You'll never believe this, but she just sat there, so calm, and when we finished she looked at us and said she knew it was haunted because she SAW the ghost!"

"She saw it?" I asked, surprised.

"Yes, she saw it," she continued. "She told us that she has seen ghosts and spirits all her life and that we had the ghost of a little African-American girl in old-fashioned clothes in our office. She was looking for someone to play with and she liked one of the rooms on the second floor. The room she liked was one we used for storage. She went on to say that if we let the ghost have the room and gave her some kind of toy to play with and acknowledged her from time to time that she would probably stop playing with our things."

"So what did you do? Did you try it?" I asked.

"Yes!" she answered excitedly. "We cleared out that room and told her it was hers and then we left a doll on the stairs for her. I didn't think it would work, but it did! The weird thing is, the doll disappeared from the stairs. At first I thought the cleaning people moved it, but when I talked to them, they said they didn't know what I was talking about. A few days later, the doll was back, but it was on the upstairs landing, just like a child had dropped it when she'd gotten distracted or something! Isn't that amazing?"

"It sounds like you found a way to co-exist with your ghostly resident," I said to her.

"Yes, we did," she replied. "You were right about the ghost. She just wanted some attention."

The origin and identity of this little girl ghost was never discovered to my knowledge. The office was formerly a private home, so the girl could have been a resident there at one time.

The reference to old-fashioned clothes got me wondering, though. Through my research on haunted locations, I have run into so many places that were either known or suspected as being part of the Underground Railroad. The reason for this is because of its location—close to the Delaware state line. Believe it or not, Delaware was a slave state. Since Pennsylvania was a free state, crossing that border got the slaves close to freedom. In addition, a large part of the population of this part of Pennsylvania were Quakers, who provided assistance and support to those escaping slavery.

As we know from history, escaping slavery was not easy. It was a long, hard journey to freedom. Many of the slaves never made it due to injury or illness. If a slave died on the journey to freedom, he or she would have had to be buried secretly to keep the railroad routes and stops from being discovered. If there is something I have learned from investigating hauntings, an unmarked grave or an unfulfilled goal, or in this case both, have been known to cause the spirit of a deceased person to remain with us.

Fortunately, in this case, whether the little girl is a former resident or a runaway slave, it seems that she has been fortunate in that she is able to reside happily with her corporeal housemates.

Chapter 19

The Ticking Tomb

Landenberg, Pennsylvania

It was a dark and stormy night. Really, it was. It had been raining all day and it was very windy and dark as we set off

London Tract Church building.

towards Delaware to look for the headless horseman of Welsh Tract Church. Needless to say, we didn't find him. We were cold, miserable, and disappointed; although what we would have done had we actually seen the headless horseman, I don't know—but we weren't ready to go home yet.

Suddenly John, the driver on our little expedition announces, "I know where the Ticking Tomb Place is. We could go there." The Ticking Tomb sounded vaguely familiar to me. Fortunately, Faith, the other investigator on this trip said, "That's the place in one of the haunted Delaware books, right? There was a legend about a little boy who ate a watch or something and you can still hear it ticking if you put your ear to his grave."

"Sounds interesting," I said, "But you know it has to be a legend. I mean, that can't possibly be true. A watch wouldn't stay in your body and keep on ticking for over a hundred years, right?" I looked back at Faith, whose real job is nursing, and she nodded. "No, it wouldn't. Let's go see it anyway, though, since we didn't find the horseman."

So off we headed to the Ticking Tomb. The "tomb" turned out to be located in a small graveyard in a little old church property at the end of a long, dark, windy road. At least the atmosphere and setting was spooky! According to the legend, the ticking tomb is right next to a heart-shaped marker. It is flat and is inscribed only with initials. We headed into the cemetery, searching for the heart-shaped marker.

The cemetery is so small, it wasn't hard to find. There was an old, heart-shaped marker, and right next to it, a flat stone with just initials carved on it. Of course, we all wanted to go first to have a listen. I honestly don't remember who went first. When it was my to step up to hear, I placed my ear against the clammy stone—and there it was! *Tick, tick, tick!* I was so excited until I realized it was *my* watch. So much for the ticking tomb. I couldn't believe we drove all over the place and slogged through a muddy old cemetery so I could hear my watch tick! Not that

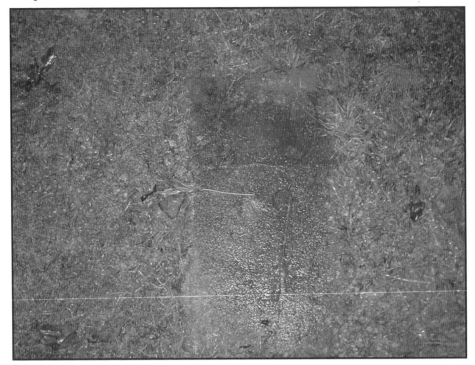

The Ticking Tomb.

we were really expecting to hear the ticking from the tomb, but it would have been nice. Faith even went back to the car to get her stethoscope out of her backpack so we could really listen. We each tried it. Nothing. Not even one *tick*.

Voices From Beyond

Since this evening was turning out to be such a bust, we decided to just walk around the little cemetery and church. The graves were old and some of them had interesting inscriptions. John decided to try to record an EVP, hoping maybe that would pick up a ticking sound.

For those that don't know, EVP is an acronym for "Electronic Voice Phenomena." These are voices of spirits or sounds from beyond that are captured on tape. Investigators use all types of audio recording devices to capture these sounds and voices, which are not audible during recording. They are only audible when played back. Usually an investigator will ask a series of questions, such as "What is your name?" in hopes of provoking a response from any spirits present.

The question that excited us that night was me asking, "Does anyone want to talk to us?" I got a frantic phone call from John at about 2 am when he was listening to the playback from his recording. "You have to hear this!" he babbled excitedly into the phone. Exhausted from a long, dreary, and somewhat disappointing night, I said, "Can't you just send it to me?"

"No!" he replied, hurt that I wasn't thrilled to bits at being awoken from a sound sleep to hear his recording. "You have to hear it. It's really clear."

"Okay," I sighed, knowing that it was easier to just give in. Also, I was a little more awake now and more than a little intrigued.

I heard the click of the playback starting. Then I heard my voice: "Does anyone want to talk to us?"

Then, amazingly, I heard a man's voice answer. It said, very clearly, "I want to talk to you about that." This voice was not John's voice. John has a very distinct voice. There were no other men at the location with us.

"Did you hear it?" John asked

"Yes," I answered, amazed. I am always amazed at EVPs. There is something so profound about hearing a voice on playback that you know you didn't hear when taping and that is clearly not the voice of anyone present.

So the night wasn't a complete bust. Good EVPs, like other good things in life, are very difficult to get. Although we did not hear ticking from the ticking tomb, we did discover an audible otherworldly presence in the cemetery of London Tract Church—and one who wanted to talk to us!

Chapter 20

Duffy's Cut

Next to the Railroad Tracks near Malvern

I first learned about Duffy's Cut from an article in the newspaper. I was surprised that I had never heard of it before. At first it was hard to find information about it. The newspaper article mentioned that a professor by the name of William Watson at Immaculata College had seen a ghost—or rather ghosts. In the *Daily Times* article by Lois Puglionesi, Professor Watson described his experience with the ghosts of Duffy's Cut.

> *"He and a friend were looking out a window one night when he noticed odd lights shining on the lawn. 'What am I looking at?' he asked Watson. ...as they watched, the radiance suddenly vanished and the scene outside the window went dark. 'I don't know what we saw. It was there and vanished. I don't believe in ghosts or aliens. But I do believe there could be some attempt to reach out, said Watson.'"*

When Watson began researching the history of the area, he discovered that there was a long tradition of ghost sightings in the area. The *Daily Times* article recounts an interview from 1889 with an area resident called Sasche:

"This resident insisted he had seen the Irishmen's ghosts dancing on their grave as he walked along the tracks one night, about a month after they died. 'It's true Mister, it was awful. They looked as if they were a kind of green and blue fire, and there they were a hopping and bobbing on their graves. ... I was too scared to run, and there I stood a knocking my knees together and the ghosts advancing and groaning all the time." And rest assured, the gentleman insisted that he 'hadn't been drinking no whiskey either.'"

It is obvious from Sasche's account that the ghosts were believed to be those of the Irish immigrants. The ghosts had not been seen there before, just since that group of Irish immigrants was buried unceremoniously in a mass grave during the cholera outbreak of 1832.

The story of Duffy's Cut is a sad one. Duffy's Cut is named for Philip Duffy, the man who contracted the job from the railroad. He was apparently in the habit of convincing able-bodied men from his home country of Ireland to emigrate and work on the railroad for him. He wasn't really doing them much of a favor. The work was hard and the living conditions were harsh. The amount of money he offered to pay them, fifty cents a day was exploitative, but it was 1832, and times were hard in Ireland, too.

In the summer of that year, Mr. Duffy brought fifty-seven Irish immigrants out to "cut" a path for the new Pennsylvania Railroad tracks being laid to Philadelphia. It was a bad summer for everyone. It was very hot and then there was a cholera epidemic. Cholera is a bacterial disease that one catches from infected water. Back then, there was no treatment for it and victims became dehydrated and died.

When the first men fell ill, they asked for help from people who lived nearby. Fear of the disease, as well as mistrust of the Irish, caused all doors to close in their faces. They were left to die. They did finally receive some assistance from the blacksmith and the Sisters of Mercy, but it was too little, too late. Sources state that the blacksmith decided to bury the workers in a common unmarked grave without receiving any burial rites. I doubt that this is entirely true. If the Sisters were there, I am sure that they administered some form of last rites or prayers over the dead.

According to Watson, at a speaking engagement that I attended at the Springfield Township Building, he suspects that the men may not have all died of cholera. He feels they may have been buried alive while in comatose states or even murdered by vigilantes who blamed them for the outbreak.

I pointed an interesting irony at that point. The Irish at the time were generally viewed as being dirty, drunken criminals. The irony is that if they *had* been drinking alcohol, they likely would not have caught cholera, since cholera is caught by drinking infected *water*.

The lack of specifics regarding the location of the burial site was frustrating, as there was no way of telling where along the tracks the unmarked grave might be. I set out on weekends, trying to locate the area. It was difficult because much of the tracks ran behind private homes. I was reduced to walking the tracks and hoping that I might, by chance, pick up on something while at the same time avoiding being hit by a commuter train. It was not an easy task. I had nearly given up when, all of a sudden, the story broke all over the place.

Excavating for the Truth

Professor Watson, who had seen the ghosts, had conducted his own research and found the location of the immigrants' camp. He was conducting an archaeological dig on the site and petitioning the state to have a historical marker placed there. The dig was started, the sign was placed, and then the story died out again. At least now I had something to go on. I looked for the marker. If I could find the marker, the section of tracks would be close by.

I dragged my husband out with me on a freezing cold New Year's Night to hunt for the location. We followed the road from the marker down toward the tracks. It looked promising, as all the streets in the development had Irish names. Then we hit the end. The tracks were obviously somewhere behind the development. To get there, we would have to walk through someone's backyard in the pitch blackness and hope we didn't fall off a cliff or run into a guard dog. I was ready to chance it, having waited so long to find it, but he was able to talk me into returning during the day when we could see where we were going and wouldn't be mistaken for prowlers.

On my return trip, I was able to bring one of my psychic investigators and two of my camera people. I couldn't wait. I was finally going to see it!

It was a bright, clear day, and when we got to the area, I could see right away where to go. There was a grassy area with a path that went down into the woods towards the tracks. I wasn't sure if it was private property or not, and I probably would have gone in anyway, but luck was on my side and as we were walking up to the path, a woman with a large, friendly dog came out of the woods. We said hello and introduced ourselves. She told us to go ahead down to the site, it was no problem. She even gave us directions as to which way to go on the paths. We were on our way!

The path ended at a walled-in enclosure with a sign above it. We looked around a bit at the enclosure, which was right next to the railroad tracks—but I wasn't feeling anything. Neither was Faith, the other psychic investigator.

I was feeling pulled to the right of the monument, down the tracks a little bit. I told the group I felt like there was something over the hill and I wanted to see what was there. As I topped the crest of the hill, I could see down into a steep valley that was obviously the site of an archaeological dig.

"This has to be it! I read that they were going to start digging to look for the camp site and the unmarked grave," I announced.

We walked gingerly down the slope towards the site. At the bottom, there was a stream that ran through a culvert under the tracks. I was thinking that if I was going to set up a camp, it would be in a place like this, next to a water source.

I didn't feel the graves were there, though. I felt the graves were over farther towards the tracks. I also did not feel that there was just one grave. I felt like there were a few of them—two graves with one or two people in them, another larger grave with more people, and possibly another with several people.

As I sat down for a while on the slope, I tried to get a feel for what they wanted. I didn't feel an unhappy feeling from this place. The feeling that I had was more of a feeling of recognition, like the fact that their deaths and their graves were never marked. There was some worry and regret that their families

The misleading site, marked with a sign.

did not know what happened to them and probably thought they just forgot about them.

We didn't get photographic evidence of the spirits, but I was left with a strong sense that they were glad that people came there

and were aware that they lived and died there. The only thing that they wanted was, of all things, whiskey! I mentioned this to the others, who also though this was unusual, but that was what I got. As we left, we talked about our feelings, and we all pretty much said the same thing. We were surprised by how peaceful it seemed, and how the main impression we got was that they were glad someone was there and knew who they were!

And the Story Continues...

Over the next couple of years, I kept up with the latest developments at Duffy's Cut. As of August 2007, they had located two graves and were planning to try and do DNA testing to find relatives of the deceased. It has also been said that any unearthed remains will be reinterred at Laurel Hill Cemetery.

Actual site of Workers' Camp at Duffy's Cut.

I think the spirits are happy enough now that their lives and deaths have been acknowledged.

The artifacts that were discovered during excavation of the immigrants' camp site were on display at the Immaculata College Library. Some of the things that we saw at Watson's speaking engagement included pipes, buckles, and tools. Although they make for an interesting link with the past tragedy, in an article by Alexis Grilli, published in the *Suburban Advertiser* on April 8, 2005, since the items were placed on display, "reports have been coming in from Immaculata's library about odd occurrences. There have been stories of knocking on doors and windows, television sets turning on and off and changing channels."

What are the ghosts trying to tell the library employees? Perhaps the ghosts that are making themselves known at the library are not the ghosts of the immigrants but are resident spirits that have something to add to the story. Maybe a trip to the library exhibit is in order…

Conclusion

If you decide to travel around the Brandywine Valley in search of some of the ghostly residents you have been introduced to in this book, keep in mind that the ghosts of this area can be anywhere. They occupy businesses, private homes, and public historic sites. They may even be found in the halls of some historic building or in the back yards of homes in a new development, much like the current "living" residents of the Valley.

The picturesque countryside that invited the early settlers to make their homes here, and that later captured the imagination and inspired the creativity of the Wyeths, still draws visitors from all over the U.S. and the world. Is it any wonder that those who lived and died in the Brandywine Valley found it difficult to leave?

These ghostly inhabitants are as much a part of the Brandywine Valley as the people and places that we see there today. So keep an eye out for these unseen residents—they add the real magic to this area.

Bibliography and Selected Resources

Adams, Charles III. *Ghost Stories of Delaware County.* Wyomissing, PA: Exeter House Books, 2005.

Adams, Charles III. *Ghost Stories of Chester County.* Wyomissing, PA: Exeter House Books, 2001.

Court Case: July 1991, Commonwealth of Pennsylvania v. Jason L. Enders, et al, 407 Pa. Superior Ct. 201, Conviction Affirmed.

Frizzell, Michael A. and George F. Walls. *Stalking The Mysterious Lights.* Originally published in *Pursuit Magazine,* Volume 20, Fourth Quarter, 1987.

Futhey, J. Smith and Gilbert Cope. *History of Chester County, Pennsylvania, with Genealogical and Biographical Sketches*, Philadelphia, Louis H. Everts, 1881.

Hoffman, Elizabeth. *In Search of Ghosts.* Philadelphia, PA: Camino Books, 1992.

Bibliography

Horn, Pamela. *The Rise and Fall of the Victorian Servant.* New York: St. Martin's, 1975, p. 17, 18.

Okonowicz, Ed. *Up the Back Stairway.* Elkton, MD: Myst & Lace Publishers, Incorporated, 1999

Religious sects and movements of magic in Italy, pg.117. Text available at: http://www.sisde.it/gnosis/Rivista5.nsf/ServNavig/26.

The Dictionary of Daily Wants—1858-1859.

Township of Birmingham, Chester County PA, Scenic Roads of Birmingham Township, www.birminghamtownship.org/scenicbyways/photos-text.pdf, 2005.

Selected Internet Resources

http://philadelphia.about.com/cs/halloween/a/haunted_phila_2.htm)
http://wintersteel.proboards26.com/
http://www.chaddsfordinn.com
http://www.crierinthecountry.com
http://www.delcohistory.org
http://www.duffyscut project.com
http://www.harrisinteractive.com/harris_poll/index.asp?PID=359
http://www.kennetthouse.com/
http://www.mystandlace.com
http://www.newlingristmill.org/newlinfamily/genealogy.htm
http://www.stjohns-concord.org/
http://www.thornbury.org/page2.html
http://www.willyoubelieve.com/concord_large.avi.